WHAT ST. PAUL SAID

or

The Teaching of St. Paul

What St. Paul Said

or

The Teaching of St. Paul

by

J. W. C. WAND

BISHOP OF LONDON

Geoffrey Cumberlege

OXFORD UNIVERSITY PRESS

LONDON   NEW YORK   TORONTO

1952

Oxford University Press,   Amen House,   London E.C.4

GLASGOW NEW YORK TORONTO MELBOURNE WELLINGTON
BOMBAY CALCUTTA MADRAS CAPE TOWN

Geoffrey Cumberlege, Publisher to the University

227V
W181

119094

PRINTED IN GREAT BRITAIN BY
EBENEZER BAYLIS AND SON, LTD., THE
TRINITY PRESS, WORCESTER, AND LONDON

Preface

THE substance of the first four chapters of this book was delivered as Lectures during the Lent of 1950 to day-school teachers under the auspices of the London County Council. The lectures were delivered extempore and taken down by a stenographer. Such revision as they have enjoyed has not departed very far from the conversational manner originally adopted. The present book form has allowed room for the addition of Chapter V to make a more rounded whole.

The purpose of the lectures was simply to give a bird's-eye view of the teaching of St. Paul as presented in his epistles, and to clarify it wherever necessary. This means essentially a detailed analysis of the documents. The analysis can easily be followed either in the Greek or in any version. I have, however, used my own translation, as given in my *New Testament Letters* (O.U.P., 3rd edition, 1947), both because of its unconventional style and also because its captions give a ready guide to the subject-matter.

I should like to thank my friend, Prebendary A. J. G. Hawes, Ph. D., for his kindness in reading the proofs.

1951   ✠ Wm: Londin:

Contents

CHAPTER I

The Background

THE object of this book is to summarize what St. Paul has said in his Epistles, so that one can get a clearer view both of the man and of his teaching. We want, if possible, to get in touch with his mind.

Letters are a particularly revealing form of auto-biography. Especially is that the case when the writer combines so thoroughly the characteristics of the extrovert and the introvert as did St. Paul. We cannot, however, get the most out of letters, just because they are letters and not treatises, unless we put them into their historical setting. Merely to take the letter out of its context and to consider it in the abstract is to lose a great deal of the tone and temper of it. Therefore before we can begin to study St. Paul's Epistles we ought first to consider the circumstances of his time, then to run rapidly through the events of his life until he began to write; and finally to set each letter in its own historical circumstances. Thus we shall be able to consider its teaching against its own individual background.

First, then, what we have to do is to deal with the contemporary situation. And here we have to notice straight away that St. Paul was a Jew by race and a Roman citizen by birth. That of course comes out quite clearly in his two names: the name Saul belongs to his Jewish race, the name Paul belongs to his Roman citizenship. (It is not generally accepted to-day that the names belong each to a separate period of his life, but it is believed that they existed always, side by side, and that as a Jew he was known as Saul and as a Roman by the name of Paul.) For us the main thing is that he was obviously a denizen of two worlds and the heir of two national characters. That was not an uncommon thing. The best known philosopher of the period, for instance, the aged Philo, who was a great teacher in Alexandria, was a Jew by race, but also a Greek by learning and culture.

Unfortunately this fact of the duality of St. Paul has made it inevitable that in studies of him one side should be made to suffer at the expense of the other. Until recently it was no uncommon thing for scholars to deal with him almost entirely from the classical point of view. Most great English theologians had been brought up in the classical tradition, and it was natural for them to treat St. Paul as a Greek. To-day we realize the mistake so thoroughly that many have gone to the other extreme and begun to treat him as a Jewish Rabbi. I personally believe that both these tendencies are wrong. St. Paul is neither one nor the other, but both. It is true that he does not stand precisely half-way; he is nearer the Jewish than the Greek end of the line; more the rabbi than the philosopher. St. Paul never reasons without reference to authority. He lays down the law like a teacher, and a Jewish teacher at that. However, because there is this double element in his character we must consider both sides of his heritage.

First, then, the pagan element. Rome at this period was mistress of Palestine as of the whole civilized world. That supremacy had been on the whole beneficial. Rome had made peace for the world, and her Emperor, Augustus, was known throughout the East as Saviour. Many people even in the West thought he had a good right to the title, and would rather have given it to him than to the Christ. The Romans not only made peace, but they also made roads, and established a system of communication between all the important towns round the Mediterranean. This was extremely important in the life of St. Paul. When he began to write letters, they could be sent by messengers with the same security as we feel to-day; and this is not true of many periods of history.

The language spoken by educated people was Greek. Paul was bilingual: he spoke Greek but we also know that to the Jews in Jerusalem he spoke Aramaic.[1] That was the common tongue used by Hebrew people in Palestine. He wrote in the Greek language, and the Septuagint, the Greek Old Testament, was his Bible.

With regard to pagan religion and thought we have to notice that this was the period of the twilight of the classical gods and also of the classical philosophy. Neither pagan religion nor philosophy at the period was practised in anything like the earlier purity. So far had they dwindled from their former influence that people had commonly become the slaves of a double fear, the fear of the unknown and the fear of death. There was a great longing for immortality and for a formal holiness that would guarantee that immortality. In order to assuage their fears and gain control of the situation people turned from the old classical religion and cultivated theosophy, theurgy and magic. They were in the grip of fate and in order to get free they must somehow bring the supernatural powers under their dominance. No spiritual authorities promised immortality more freely than did the great religions of the East. In

---

[1] Acts xxi. 40; xxii. 2.

consequence at that period there was a surge of Eastern
religions into the West. It was expressed in the well-
known phrase 'the Orontes has flowed into the Tiber'.[1]
What fascinated people about Eastern religions was their
mysterious quality. Their variety was very great and their
detailed practices extremely fascinating for the super-
stitious. They were built upon the one common factor of
the birth, death and rebirth of nature in the constantly
revolving cycle of the seasons. That constant renewal
seemed to give a suggestion of immortality. Some saviour
god was associated with this process, and the object of the
cult was to put the believer into so close a union with that
saviour that with him the initiate might hope to emerge
into rebirth and so be guaranteed a life beyond the
grave.

One of the most canvassed questions of our day is how
far St. Paul was associated with this type of thought. His
view of the Sacraments is sometimes alleged to be derived
from it. I think almost everyone to-day is agreed that the
Christian Sacraments could not have been borrowed direct
from the mystery cults. That does not mean that the cults
could have had no influence at all in the development of
Christian thought and practice: we are influenced even by
that against which we react most violently. What it does
mean is that there was spread throughout the religious
society of the day a belief in the capacity of material things
to convey an unseen and possibly spiritual power. The
sharp distinction between spirit and matter as we draw it,
perhaps wrongly, to-day was not then generally recognized.
In any case that gives us the explanation of a good deal
St. Paul says about the Sacraments, and particularly about

[1] Said by Juvenal (the Roman satirist, c. A.D. 55–127).

baptism as a 'grafting into Christ'. It may encourage us not to minimize suggestions that lie in St. Paul's words, but to take what he says at its face value.

These mystery cults were not the only example of clubs and societies that occupied time and attention at this period. Every small body of people who had a common interest developed a club in which they would meet each other in order to further it, much as we do to-day. There were benefit clubs of every kind, which arose legitimately under Roman government, however worried it might be at the suggestion of a secret society. Even a local church might claim exemption from surveillance on the ground that it was a burial club.

The state religion of the period was of course nothing at all like this. That was merely intended to subserve the needs of imperial unity. It was not strictly speaking a religion at all, but was almost purely a formal matter. To throw some grains of incense on the altar before the statue of Cæsar was like standing up in the theatre when you hear 'God Save the King'. Such a state religion offered very remarkable tolerance for all other sorts of religion. The idea that Rome persecuted Christianity because it was intolerant of any religion other than its own is wrong. It would put up with almost any other cult so long as its own was not flouted. Without that tolerance St. Paul would have fared much more hardly than he actually did.

So much for the pagan side. Now a word about the Jewish. Palestine was under the suzerainty of the Roman power and that power was represented by Procurators. Pilate was Procurator from A.D. 6 to 37, Felix from 52 and Festus from 57. These Procurators had a very considerable amount of power, but so far as possible, where there was a native prince, they allowed him to carry on under their supervision. Such a prince, Antipas, was deposed because he tried to usurp a greater dignity than they were prepared to allow him. Agrippa I reigned from 37 to 44, having under him Iturea, Galilee, Samaria and Judea, all of which he had got as gifts from the Emperors Caligula and Claudius. He was well in with the Roman power and thus managed to build up a Jewish empire and to restore the boundaries of the territory over which his father Herod the Great had ruled.

One interesting point is that when Agrippa succeeded in 37, the town of Damascus was placed under the sovereignty of another native prince, Aretas, a fact that was important, as we shall see, in the story of St. Paul. Agrippa II was too young to succeed when Agrippa I died in 44, but in 53 he was given Iturea to make a start and then Nero gave him other seats in Galilee and Peraea. It was he who actually finished the great Temple in Jerusalem. Like all the Herods, he tried in his own way to combine Judaism and Hellenism. That ambition can be judged from his interest in great buildings, another version of the same process that we have seen exemplified at higher levels in Philo and Paul.

The religious centre of Judaism was the Temple, which was restored by Herod the Great and finished by Agrippa II. There all the sacrifices were offered and the ceremonial law fulfilled. But one has a feeling that to a very large extent the spiritual life had gone out of the sacrificial system. One thing the Temple did for St. Paul was to stamp in his mind most clearly the difference between Jew and Gentile. The Court of Israel was separated from the Court of the Gentiles by a stone wall on which was placed a notice that any Gentile penetrating beyond it would be punished by death. Real religion seems to have centred much more in the synagogue. There were no sacrifices, but psalms, readings and prayers—what we should call a choir office. These synagogues had started in embryo as far back as the period of the Exile when the Jews had no temple, but had developed this type of service as a substitute. In later days the synagogues derived a special importance from the dispersion of the Jews. Throughout practically the whole of the civilized world there were Jewish colonies. For each there would be one or more synagogues. In these little gatherings they would be able to study the Law, reading their scriptures and worshipping as their forefathers had done before them. They each recognized the authority of the Great Synagogue, the Sanhedrin, in Jerusalem; while the lesser synagogues in the city formed a home for many returning colonists to whom the Temple represented little of practical importance, even if it was the ritual centre of the whole cult.

As is well known, the Jews were divided into a number of sects. The Sadducees were conservative in religion, sticking to the letter of the old law. The Pharisees were the liberal element allowing discussion of the law and bringing in reason to apply its regulations to all the details of everyday life. These findings were summarized in the Halakah, what we should call common law. This was capable of being indefinitely developed, and made it possible to adapt the stiff letter of the law to the changing circumstances of every day. St. Paul was himself a Pharisee and had sat at the feet of the great teacher Gamaliel. In addition to these two well-known sects there was that of the Essenes. They combined to some extent the belief and practice of Judaism with the kind of life characteristic of the mystery cults. They had common meals and indulged in sacred ablutions, and they endeavoured to live the life of an established order, both moral and ceremonial. But because they were a retiring folk it is probable they had a very small influence on the life of the people as a whole.

That, in the briefest outline, is the background of St. Paul. We have now to place in perspective some of the details of his life, bringing it down to the time when he began to write his letters.

He was born about A.D. 6. His parents were Jews and his father was in all probability a freed slave. If you ask why one says that, the answer is that it is the easiest way of explaining how he got his privileges as a Roman citizen. The city in which his family lived and where he was born was Tarsus, which had by turns been an Oriental, a Greek and a Roman city. It was especially favoured both by Antony and by Augustus. They made it a free city, and they had also given it the privilege of a free harbour, so that it not only managed to a very large extent its own affairs, a matter about which St. Paul was very proud, but it also had rights in the fixing of customs and taxation. It was the centre of imperial interests in the district and had also a university of such importance as to vie with Athens. The philosopher Athenodorus taught there. He lived to be 92, and it is possible that St. Paul may have seen him and heard him lecture. Athenodorus was a great Stoic and set the tone, not only for studies in the university, but also for local politics in the city. If ever there was a government which came near to Plato's ideal of a philosopher king, it was to be found in Tarsus, because its philosophers played a really important part in its management. The result was a restrictive aristocracy. Control was in the hands of a few people who held the rights of citizenship. Of them Paul was one, and that no doubt explains his great pride in his native city and his Roman citizenship.

Nevertheless Judaism was his dominating passion. As a young man he went to Jerusalem, and became the rising hope of the Pharisees. As such he took a leading part in the attack on the Christians. Then when the persecution was stopped, largely owing to the influence of the Roman authorities, he looked round for some other place where he could go and carry on the war against the heretics. He thought of Damascus, which had just come under the authority of the prince Aretas. He got permission to go there, where there would be less likelihood of Roman interference. But it was on that road in the year 37 (the date is a little doubtful) that he was converted.

Everyone knows the story of that conversion and nobody can give a satisfactory account of it without assuming divine intervention. However, it gives some evidence of a state of nervous tension to which St. Paul was possibly subject. It has been suggested that his 'thorn in the flesh' implies that he was an epileptic. If that was so, he shared his disability, as Nock has pointed out, with King Alfred the Great and Napoleon. Average people seldom make great leaders, and we must expect to find something extraordinary in the psychological make-up of St. Paul.[1] At any rate all his life through he must have been conscious of a tension in his own mental condition.

[1] See A. D. Nock, *St. Paul* (Home University Library).

He must have thought a great deal about his neighbours who were not Jews. He had attacked Christians because they were making an approach to such people by declaring the supersession of the Jewish law. For that reason he had assisted in the execution of Stephen, and when a psychological shock came, it was precisely that terrible event and its implications, against which he had been struggling subconsciously all the time, that rose to the surface of his consciousness and made him aware of the revolt at the root of his being. From that moment the dominating influence in his life was the voice of the Christ which had spoken to him from Heaven and which he interpreted as a definite command, bidding him change his allegiance and minister to the Gentiles.

For a time he wandered uncertainly about the Nabatæan portion of Arabia, and then with his mind made up returned to Damascus. In all probability he began at once to address himself to the Gentiles, and for that reason aroused considerable opposition; and was compelled to flee. The native prince had been warned of what had happened and had set a cordon about the gates. Paul had to be let down the city wall in a basket so that he could escape. He seems to have spent two years in isolation wandering about from place to place, but in the year 39 he paid a visit to Jerusalem. The purpose was to see Peter and James, the leaders of the Apostolic band, no doubt with the hope of getting himself recognized by central authority.

After a fortnight's preaching under the protection of Barnabas he had to face a fresh outburst. He was thereupon sent to Tarsus and preached for some time in Syria and Cilicia. That seems to be the best reading of the facts as we gather them from a combination of Galatians and the Acts of the Apostles. In the year 46 he paid a second visit to Jerusalem. That was at the end of a year's missionary teaching in Antioch in the company of Barnabas. Agabus, the prophet, had announced the certainty of an approaching world-wide famine. The prospect was regarded with very considerable concern by the Christians in Antioch because it was recognized that the 'poor saints' in Jerusalem, who had been pooling their resources and living on the capital, would find it extremely difficult to keep body and soul together. Consequently Barnabas and Paul decided to go up to Jerusalem and take with them what they had been able to collect for the benefit of the Christians there. That is mentioned quite naturally by Acts but not by St. Paul, although of course he often speaks of his interest in the relief question. The reason for his silence is probably that St. Paul on that occasion simply went as an agent taking financial assistance. When his business was done he must have returned immediately, and had no time for those discussions about Christian practice in relation to Gentiles which formed the object of a later visit; and so no mention was made of this occasion when he wrote his Epistle to the Galatians, which after all is concerned mainly with the Gentile question.

After his return to Antioch there came the arrangements for his first missionary journey, which lasted from 46 to 49. The reason for this new departure was that the Christians in Antioch, under the influence of Barnabas, realized what a great opportunity there was for spreading the gospel. They had found in Antioch that though they could not often convert the Jews they made a great success with the

Gentile proselytes, some of whom had become Jews by the rite of circumcision, but others of whom were mere hangers-on of the synagogues. To the latter Christianity came as glad news, announcing an opportunity to enter into a new and ideal life without having to forfeit their own nationality and become adopted members of the Jewish people. It was to minister to such converts that Barnabas had fetched Paul to Antioch. The work thus undertaken had been interrupted by the visit to Jerusalem, and it was not long after the return of the two friends to Antioch that the leaders there determined under the guidance of the Holy Spirit to send them off again to extend their work further afield.

It was that kind of thing that St. Paul had in mind when he started on his first missionary journey. He and Barnabas made their first big effort in Cyprus, where the proconsul Sergius Paulus was converted and Elymas the sorcerer suffered blindness because he resisted. From there they went on to Antioch in Pisidia where occurred a momentous innovation. It was brought about by an attack from the Jews who had found that the proselytes were beginning to follow Paul and Barnabas. The two turned on their opponents: 'We have appealed to you; we had hoped you would become members of the New Israel and accept Jesus as the Messiah; but seeing that you have refused the gospel we will turn henceforth to the Gentiles.' It is possible that Paul did not realize the full implications of this action, but it was a complete change of approach and it meant that henceforth the gospel would be addressed to the Gentiles directly, and not through the medium of Judaism.

After leaving Pisidian Antioch he and his friend went to

Iconium, and then to Lystra, where they healed the cripple and the people began to worship them. That ended in another attack by the Jews, and Paul was barely rescued from a death by stoning. Soon after that the missionaries doubled on their tracks and returned to their base at Antioch in Syria.

We have Paul then in Antioch in the year 49, and there he put into practice at home what he had already begun in the mission field, that is to say, he preached the gospel freely to the Gentiles. There were two consequences of this, one organizational and the other psychological. On the organizational level it meant that those who were converted by his teaching could be admitted into the Christian Church on the mere profession of faith in Christ followed by baptism. They did not have to pass through the gate of Judaism and be circumcised. Therefore the Christian Church was now obviously disentangled from the Jewish Church. It was no longer a narrow circle of special believers in the midst of a larger whole. The Christian Church was henceforth an organization on its own, standing by itself, with no outer circle to be penetrated before admission could be gained to its ranks.

From the point of view of church organization there never has been a more important step taken since its foundation. The move was equally important on psychological grounds. It meant that henceforth there was a clear doctrine of the conditions required for salvation. Obviously you could not make sure of eternity by observing a particular series of regulations. The law was not capable of ensuring salvation. In place of that law there was demanded a psychological attitude, an attitude of faith and trust and an open heart towards God, willing to receive gladly His free gift. Salvation was something you could not earn in any way whatever: you could only accept it as a benefaction. It was a staggering blow to human pride to feel you could not merit a place in God's redemption but must just receive it like a child at the hand of your Father.

Naturally there was a great outcry in Antioch about the whole question, especially when 'certain men came down from Judea and taught the brethren, "Except ye be circumcised ye cannot be saved".' Finally Barnabas and Paul with Titus went up to Jerusalem to see if they could get a decision at headquarters about it. This visit is recorded in two different places. Acts xv gives an account of all the proceedings step by step. After much discussion among the Apostles and elders agreement was reached. Paul and Barnabas were allowed to pursue their mission to the Gentiles without demanding circumcision. But in order that there should be freedom of contact between Jews and Gentiles they were asked to secure obedience to these simple rules: Gentile converts must keep free from sexual offences; they must not eat meat sacrificed to idols; they must abstain from blood and from things strangled. If we remind ourselves how immoral was much of pagan society at that time, we shall understand how necessary were some such regulations if Jew and Gentile were to mix freely in each other's homes. Also the Gentiles must be careful about regulations with regard to food. They must see that there was nothing but 'kosher' food on their table such as Jews could eat. In the same way they must take care that they did not bring into their common meals food which had been used in pagan ceremonies and then sold in the market-place.

In Galatians ii we are given St. Paul's own account of the proceedings in Jerusalem, and that differs in some respects from the account given in Acts xv. What St. Paul tells us is that the Apostles gave him and Barnabas *carte blanche* for their mission to the Gentiles. He is emphatic that he received no sort of dictation from the leaders in Jerusalem and he makes no mention of the regulations. It is at first sight difficult to reconcile these two accounts. It is possible, however, that Paul and Barnabas were not actually present at the Council. They may have dealt directly with the leading Apostles, Peter, James and John, and decided as far as they could on the lines to be laid down for the future, while the actual Council may have been held after Paul himself had left. In that case Paul would not necessarily be very familiar with the code of manners agreed upon, and it is possible that he never accepted it. The curious thing is that although he often deals with this kind of situation he never refers to the code. It may be that the omission is due to St. Paul's particular idiosyncrasy. He was not an administrator by nature but what the Americans call an inspirational leader. He cared very little for regulations. For most people it is a natural instinct, when a question of discipline arises, to get out the 'book of words' and see what the regulations say about it. St. Paul was not like that. He would never look at the 'Law' but would always go back to fundamental principles. On the other hand, whenever he found that people were acting contrary to the spirit in which these particular rules were framed he was down on them quickly enough. That happened in Antioch and with no less a person than St. Peter. Peter mixed freely with the Gentile Christians until some of the Jewish Christians made the position too hot

for him. Then he began to alter his attitude and actually
withdrew from such friendly and social contact with converted Gentiles. Thus he once again raised up that barrier
of the legal system, which St. Paul thought had been
thrown down. Paul 'accused him to his face', although
Barnabas also began to withdraw himself from contact
with the Gentile converts. There remains a real difficulty
about the situation. One does not know why the regulations were not produced. They would surely have settled
the question at once.

After this episode Paul went on his travels again, probably late in 49. With Timothy and Silas he revisited the
scenes of his former exploits in Southern Galatia and then
went on to Northern Galatia. Paul had the famous vision
at Troas when he was called to pass over to Europe. At
Philippi he first converted Lydia, and later exorcized a
soothsaying spirit. For the latter act he found himself in
prison, from which he was released after an earthquake.
He then went on to Thessalonica, where an attack was
made upon the house of Jason in which he was residing.
But Jason substituted himself for the Apostle, and Paul,
with Silas, was able to escape again. They passed on to
Berea, where they made many converts before the old
trouble was renewed; and so they arrived at Athens, where
Paul preached his famous sermon about the Unknown
God. But by this time he had begun to wonder what had
happened at Thessalonica after his hurried departure. He
sent Timothy back to find out how his converts there were
faring. He himself went on to Corinth and settled down
with Aquila and Priscilla, working at his trade and spending the rest of his time in evangelistic work. Here Timothy
came to him with a favourable report from Thessalonica.

On the receipt of this reassuring news Paul wrote with considerable relief his first Epistle to the Thessalonians. It probably represents his first essay in authorship. At any rate it is generally reckoned as the first of his extant letters.

CHAPTER II

Letters of the Second Journey

By the end of the last chapter we had followed the career of St. Paul to the point when he first took up his task of writing. Before we give the content of his letter there are two points with which we must deal.

First, his method of writing. These epistles are genuine letters; they are occasional writings referring to an immediate need and are in no way systematic. All that St. Paul has to say in them arose out of a particular situation. There is always some issue of immediate importance and of a practical character. Normally the Apostle drives the subject back to fundamental principles, and therein lies a very large part of his importance for posterity. He deals with a temporary issue in the light of eternity; the occasional element fades away and a point of fundamental importance stands out in all its clarity. Because he treats topics in that way his letters set a standard in faith, in belief, in worship, in organization for the whole of the Christian Church ever after.

The letters of course were dictated, and were actually written by an amanuensis. Sometimes Paul appends his own signature; sometimes he even writes the final message in his own hand, either to avoid suspicion of a forgery or else to lend particular emphasis to some point he wants to stress. Incidentally he jokes about the childish character of his own penmanship. He may have been shortsighted. Some people think his 'thorn in the flesh' had something to do with an affection of the eyes. Anyway he wrote in much larger characters than were customary.

One has to imagine him dictating letters in a good deal of excitement. His whole style is that of a man at the height of enthusiasm. He has no time to be careful of his grammar, or even of a broken sentence. His mind is darting about the particular point at issue without long consecutive thought, and the style in consequence is dramatic rather than literary. As far as their *genre* is concerned the epistles are rather hard to place, but they approximate most closely to that type of classical literature known as diatribes, philosophical exercises carried through in an argumentative style. Paul of course is always arguing, and that further explains the generally nervous character of his style. One imagines Paul dictating his works much as G. K. Chesterton is alleged to have done, charging about the room in the throes of composition and stabbing at the cushions as he gives the *coup de grâce* to his invisible opponent.

Second, a brief mention of the way in which the epistles found their place in the Canon. We have to remember that these are the oldest Christian writings still extant. They are of course earlier than the Gospels in their present form, and may be the first Christian writings ever to have appeared in black and white. St. Paul wrote them to particular churches and they would be read in the Christian meeting on the Sunday. In some cases, if they were circular letters, they would go round from one church to another and be read to each congregation in turn. That they were written by an Apostle gave them a special importance, particularly when that Apostle had been the first missionary in that neighbourhood. The fact that they were read in the actual services would inevitably suggest a parallel between them and the Old Testament which was normally read in the synagogue. Thus a certain sacredness would be transferred from it to them.

There were other letters, now lost to us, some perhaps by St. Paul but many certainly by other Christian leaders. One presumes that it is the best of them which have been preserved. Possibly the importance of the recipient church might give a special dignity to a particular letter and ensure its preservation. Nothing of the sort, however, would explain the retention of the epistle to Philemon. However, that is such a pure gem in itself that one hopes the contemporary Church preserved it just for that reason.

There was already a collection of Pauline letters before the New Testament Canon took shape. It is actually referred to in the Second Epistle of St. Peter (iii. 16) which suggests that Paul's letters had already been gathered into a *corpus*, and already ranks them as 'scriptures'.

When you get outside the New Testament evidence you find in the Apostolic Fathers reference to two Pauline letters. Clement of Rome (A.D. 96) wrote to Corinth and actually mentions 1 Corinthians, while Polycarp (A.D. 116), writing to Philippi, mentions the epistle to the Philippians. When you come to Justin Martyr (*c*. 150) you have the mention of a collection of apostolic writings as being read in the Christian services along with the Prophets and used as a basis of comment and exhortation. That fixes the Pauline writings in the selection of Christian scriptures already reckoned as sacred. Thenceforth their place in the Canon is secure.

We can now return to that first letter, which we left

Paul beginning to write. He is at Corinth towards the end of his second journey. He is living with Aquila and Priscilla, staying with them a year and a half and converting many people to Christianity, including Crispus, the ruler of the synagogue. Timothy has joined him and brought him a satisfactory report about the state of things in Thessalonica.

Thessalonica needs a word about the town itself. It seems to have been an extremely pleasant place, built in the form of an amphitheatre at the head of the Gulf of Salonica with hot springs in the neighbourhood, doubly a health resort. Paul, accompanied by Silas, had visited it earlier on this journey, and for three successive Sabbaths he had preached in the synagogue. He had converted a few Jews and a large number of proselytes. By so doing he had stirred up the enmity of the Jewish community, who only failed to capture him at the home of Jason because they attacked the house when he was out. He thus had an opportunity to escape, and left the town the next day.

Now Timothy has been back to the scene of these adventures and has returned to report on the fate of the Christians whom Paul had converted. They had apparently behaved very well under the persecution that had ensued, and there was no room for complaint of their fidelity and staunchness. They are, however, worried about the second coming of Christ, and they are especially troubled because they have begun to wonder what is going to happen to their friends who had embraced the faith with them but who now, through illness or old age, may begin to die off. Will dead Christians have any part in the glories of the Second Coming? Will they be able to

share in the salvation that Christ will bring at the end of
time?

1 Thessalonians is the answer to that question. St. Paul
takes the opportunity of dealing at the same time with a
few other matters relating to conduct and discipline,
practical subjects that are never far from his mind; but
the doctrine of the Parousia is the essential theme of the
letter.

1 THESSALONIANS—*The Second Coming*

i   Paul begins the first chapter with an introduction in
which he thanks God for having converted his readers,
and thanks *them* for the witness they have given to the
Christian faith. At the end of the chapter he says by way
of parenthesis that they are all waiting for the Coming,
ii   and thus sounds the main note of his thesis. In the second
chapter, however, he goes on to remind them of his visit,
of his good faith and how he proved it by taking no pay
for his ministrations, but worked with his own hands to
support himself. Now it has all been spoilt by the Jews'
persecution. They have always persecuted the prophets,
and in the present generation they persecute the Christian
17   leaders in the same way. Towards the end of chapter ii
Paul begins a fresh section, speaking about the tremendous
anxiety he has felt on his readers' behalf. Here you find
the affectionate side of Paul's character coming out
strongly. He had a constant vision of the people to whom
iii   he ministered: 'out of sight' did not mean 'out of mind'
for him. He simply had to send Timothy because he was
so worried, wondering what had happened to them after

he himself had left. He is overjoyed because Timothy has returned and assured him of their loyalty. 'I feel alive again.'

In chapter iv he says they must be careful about purity *iv* in marriage as in all other sexual relations. They must pursue the aims of love in the Christian sense of *agapē*, that is service of others. They must show that spirit particularly to the brethren as they are beginning to show it to the whole country round. Further, they must work in order that they may support themselves and not have to sponge on other people.

At verse 13 he broaches the question of the departed: *13* 'you have been asking me about Christians who have died before the Second Coming has taken place; what is to become of them?' The answer is that Jesus and His members are inseparable. You cannot divide Him from His people. That means that when He comes they will come with Him. This is the glorious truth; when His Second Coming occurs they will actually arrive with Him. And if you go on to ask 'what about us who will be still living?' the answer is that we shall be caught up to meet them in the air.

Slightly naïve, you may think, but it was a most marvellous answer to give, one we are familiar with to-day but which must have seemed epoch-making as it burst on the minds of Paul's contemporaries. If you are members of Christ you are one with Him and can never be separated from Him. Therefore when Christ comes in triumph and all Christ's own are brought together it will be to proclaim His victory and to reside with Him for ever.

Having thus started on the question of the Second *v* Advent Paul goes on to say it will be unexpected and sudden. It will of course be inevitable, in exactly the same way as the pains of a pregnant woman are inevitable. 'We are quite certain it will come, and we must be on the watch so that we may be ready when it does appear.'

12   The letter closes with an exhortation to discipline. 'Stick to your leaders. Pray constantly. Quench not the Spirit.'

That is 1 Thessalonians in the briefest digest I can give of its contents. It filled its readers with the joyful expectancy of the end. That certain of them left their daily work in order to bask in the sunshine of the imminent Coming was a proof that its teaching was almost too successful. So Paul had to write again and try to put the matter straight. In the following year, 51, he dispatched the second epistle to the Thessalonians.

2 THESSALONIANS—*The Second Coming*

i   Here again Paul begins by giving thanks for the loyalty and the mutual love so carefully maintained by his friends throughout the persecution. He also thanks God because there is guaranteed to them all in the Parousia the promise

7   of a great reward. He says that Coming will be accompanied by fire, by the punishment of all who are evil and by the triumph of the good. When Christ comes on that great day He will be glorified by His saints, among whom his readers will be numbered. Having thus started to describe the Parousia Paul goes on to clear up the prevalent

ii   misapprehensions about it. The Second Advent occupies almost the whole of chapter ii, and here he has to begin with a disclaimer. They are not to believe that the Day has already come. 'Even if you have received letters purporting to come from me to say that the Day is here, those letters were forged and you must not be led astray by them. The Day has still to come.' They will be able to know when it is about to appear, for there will be many premonitory signs. These signs are as follows: there will be a manifestation of anti-Christ which will result in a great apostasy. Many will fall away from Christ, and the faithful will see the principle of lawlessness at work in the world. Indeed they see it working in the world already, but there is a restraining power which at the moment keeps lawlessness in check.

(There is a good deal that gives rise to question here. What was this principle of lawlessness of which there had been already some manifestation? Many think it was the turbulence of the Jews who were attacking Christians in every place where Paul had raised up converts. Others hold that it was the lawlessness displayed by the Emperor Caligula, who after his severe illness was more than half mad, and was thoroughly persuaded that he was himself a god. He even wanted to have his image set up for worship in the Temple at Jerusalem. It is possible that that is what was in Paul's mind. If that is the case then in all probability the 'restraining power' is that of the reigning Roman Emperor, Claudius, who had succeeded Caligula and had given evidence of some military capacity. He did indeed support the best ideals and keep in check a great deal of the evil that might otherwise have broken loose over the Empire. That leads to the suggestion that St. Paul was afraid that when Claudius came to be suc-

ceeded by a new emperor there might be manifested a
fresh emergence of lawlessness which would bring about
the expected apostasy with all the consequent suffering of
the saints.)

9   However, a new manifestation of lawlessness will certainly occur and the Antagonist will be manifested. But
he will be destroyed by the very breath of Jesus. Behind
all this trouble can be discerned the machinations of Satan
who is working out his own schemes for the destruction of
mankind.

(In thus describing what he believes will be the signs of
the end Paul is using the kind of imagery that you get in the
apocalyptic literature of the Jews and the sort of language
you find in Bunyan's *Pilgrim's Progress.* Nevertheless he is
trying to stick as near to principle as one can in such a
matter. He uses these rather pictorial phrases in order to
point out that the end is not yet, and that there is a great
deal of trouble to be gone through before it comes. But the
end *will* come and, he insists, we can be quite sure that
in the last resort the evil will be defeated and that it will
be Jesus who will reign over all.)

13   What, then, he asks, in face of this certainty, is your
immediate duty? Your immediate duty is to thank God
and stand fast; you are the chosen people of God; you
iii   therefore will share the glory of Christ. Separate yourselves from all the disorderly elements in society; follow
6   the example I set you; you know how I worked without
accepting free hospitality. Work and earn your own living,
that alone will give you a right to be fed. Do the duty that

lies nearest to hand, and do not let yourselves be carried 11
off by hysterical excitement. If people won't adopt that
sober attitude send them to Coventry and exclude them
from your society. All the hysterical elements must be
weeded out in order that in quietness and confidence you
may establish the Church. Finally, says Paul, I write with
my own hand the concluding salutation, a guarantee of
the authenticity of every epistle. You can see that this is
my own writing and feel assured that the message is
mine.

GALATIANS (A.D. 52)–*Faith or Law, the way of Salvation?*

The Epistle to the Galatians was probably written soon
after Paul had got back to Antioch at the end of his second
journey. It is an entirely different kind of letter from the
two last. The main point there was the Second Coming.
In Galatians the fundamental point is the psychological
approach to religion. This letter arises out of a very real
difficulty, and goes right down to the root of St. Paul's
theology. The principle embodied in it is a matter of life
and death to him, nothing less.

A word first about the external circumstances of the
letter. There is a very well-known doubt about the precise
set of churches to which it was addressed. It may have
been written to the congregations in the northern part of
of the great inner plateau of Asia Minor. More likely it
was written to those in the southern part, the churches of
Pisidian Antioch, Iconium, Derbe and Lystra, in which
towns Paul had encountered the attacks we mentioned
when discussing the events of his first journey. He visited

these churches again on his second journey, and it was during this second visitation that apparently he noticed signs of defection. There had been a departure from the purity of the gospel which he had been careful to teach. The dissident movement had been started by members of the Judaizing party who expected Gentile converts to observe the Jewish law and merely to add to that observance practices which they had acquired as Christians.

As I have previously pointed out there is involved in that position a double question, of organization and of faith. Is the Christian Church just an enclave within Judaism, so that one must pass through Judaism before becoming a Christian? That is the first question, but the psychological one is much more serious and indeed quite fundamental. Is religion to be reckoned as the observance of a legal system or is it to be found in the attitude of heart and mind of the believer towards God? Wrapped up in the latter was the practical question how far was the Mosaic law an obligation for Christian Gentiles? It was a problem of legalism versus liberty, a conflict between Christ and the Law. Psychologically the difference involved a complete change in one's attitude towards the whole of life. If one accepted the view that the Law was necessary, it meant that you believed you could gain eternal salvation through your successful achievement in fulfilling it; whereas if you took the other view it meant that whatever you did you could never earn your salvation but must accept it as a gift freely offered. The contrasted attitudes of mind characteristic of these two different positions constitute the really important division in the field of religion. If you accept your salvation merely as a free gift without any hope of earning it, then you have a receptive attitude towards life, an open and responsive mind towards the good-ness that is God. If, on the other hand, you believe you can earn your salvation as a matter of merit, then the more you strive to that end the harder becomes your attitude towards God and towards everyone you meet, because it is rooted and grounded in pride. The psychological dif-ference between these two approaches is quite extra-ordinary. Paul points out to the Galatians that the question in dispute is not a matter of the fringe of religion but belonging to its very heart.

So from Syrian Antioch he wrote this letter to the churches in Galatia in order to try to make the issue clear. He had just been through that interesting experience at Corinth, when his friend Justus had been brought before Gallio. The Roman judge had dismissed the case and so in effect set the Apostle free to preach his Gospel. He could not now be challenged on the ground of Roman law. This was a salutary lesson in the meaning of liberty, and he transfers it to the sphere of religion. Freedom was of the essence of a truly religious character.

I would have liked to report that what St. Paul has tried to do in this letter is to insist that his people shall live by the terms of the Council of Jerusalem where, as we have seen, regulations were laid down to govern the social conduct of Gentile converts who were in contact with Jewish Christians. But we are not sure that St. Paul knew about these regulations, and he does not mention them at all. But in dealing with the much more fundamental principle he is at least trying to insist on the preservation of the spirit that lies behind those instructions from Jerusalem. Or perhaps we might say he is trying to make the Galatians live in the spirit of the conversations he

himself must have had with the leaders before the Council
actually took place.

i

6

10

We proceed now to the text of the letter. It begins in a
manner most unusual to St. Paul, with a serious reproach
against his readers. He complains in the bitterest tones
that what they have now accepted is a different gospel
from the one he preached. They are not manifesting belief
in the gospel as originally taught by him. He goes on to
say that his gospel came by revelation. It was given him
direct from heaven.

(That may be a reference to the vision seen near
Damascus. Or it may be characteristic of the Jewish
method of statement, particularly of the prophetic. It was
customary to refer immediate events back to first causes.
The Hebrew prophet always says, 'The Lord spake unto
me, saying . . .' He goes back to the primary cause of his
inspiration and neglects every intermediate agency. But
the interesting thing is that Paul, while following the
characteristic Jewish method of statement, is at pains to
point out that he does mean exactly what he says, and
that he is not just leaving out intermediate steps *pro forma*.
In this case his revelation does come from heaven whether
in the scene on the Damascus road or some other. He
emphasizes the fact that he spent his first three years as
a Christian in Arabia and Damascus, and even when he
went to Jerusalem he had no contact with anybody there
who could enlighten him except Peter and James, and
with them only for a fortnight.)

ii

In chapter ii he says that the circumcision question was

raised later after an interval of some fourteen years and
that he explained his position privately to the leaders in
Jerusalem. As far as he was concerned he never gave any
place to those people who, calling themselves brethren,   4
yet demanded that Gentile Christians should accept the
Jewish law. As a result of the representations he made to   6
the leaders they gladly accepted the fact that he had a
vocation to preach to the Gentiles and gave him and
Barnabas *carte blanche* to carry on with that work while
they dealt with the Jews. Paul is very vehement about that.
The only injunction laid upon him was to remember the
poor, which of course he was very glad to do.

(You get a somewhat different view if you stick to the
account in Acts. To fit them together and make one nar-
rative of the two is not easy. What we have in Galatians
is Paul's own account of what happened, and as he gives
it on oath I think we must accept his version and simply
try to fit Acts in as well as we can.)

Now, Paul goes on, an awkward situation developed   11
after I had been to Jerusalem. I went back to Antioch and
carried on preaching there. Peter arrived on a visit and
at first he lived as one of us and met all the Gentile
Christians without difficulty, until some of these same
Judaizers appeared in Antioch as emissaries from James,
and said he was doing wrong. Then Peter vacillated and
began to withdraw from all contact with the Gentile
Christians. Not only so but Barnabas also was carried
away by his example. I had to challenge Peter publicly   14
and point out how inconsistent was his conduct. What
you have to stick to is a real principle. If you once allow   17

yourself to be circumcised or yield to the Law's demands then you have denied Christ. It is either the Law or Christ; you cannot have both. But the Christian has already decided: he has died to the Law and been received to a new life in Christ. We cannot churlishly refuse the free gift of God.

iii   So in chapter iii Paul discusses the means of salvation. It is accomplished, he says, not by law but by faith. You have actually received the Spirit, and that is something quite different from the sort of spirit in which you lived before you were converted. That is a matter of actual experience. You got it as a free gift as the result of your open faith. Having thus begun in the Spirit, you cannot now want to change over to the sphere of mechanical law.

Paul had had a Jewish training and he often reasoned
7   like a Rabbi. Thus he here draws an illustration from the Old Testament. He says that this free gift of the Spirit is characteristic of the way in which God dealt with the earliest forefathers of our race. If you read the life of Abraham you will see that God gave His blessing freely in response to faith whereas what you get under the Law is a series of threats of punishment. Abraham is the real ancestor of all people who live by faith, and his special descendant to whom the blessing was promised is Christ.
13   In Him we are released from the penalties of the Law because He has already borne its full curse for our sakes.
18   We inherit only blessing. This inheritance comes to us not because it is legally entailed but because God actually promised that he would confer a blessing through Abraham. The Law was only put in temporarily to keep men straight till the promise was fulfilled. We therefore got what we have received because God had promised us. It

is the unearned gift of God. What then is the purpose of   21
the Law? Is it in conflict with the promise? The answer
is No. It was given to keep check over sin and to prevent
sin from spreading until the time should come when men
would be brought into contact with Christ and the free
life promised to Abraham and his 'seed' could burst out
in all its glory. The Law has performed the function of   22
the slave in the big household whose business it was to
take children to school and see that they did not get
attracted by the interesting sights and scenes on the way
but arrived at their destination. Unpleasant as it was,
that was the function of the Law; it kept men on the
straight path of moral conduct and prevented them from
going astray until the time should come when they would
find themselves in the presence of Christ.

However, during the period of his minority the son is   *iv*
little better than a slave. It is only later that he under-
stands the implications of sonship. The important thing
about his change of status is that he has passed from
slavery to freedom; he has been recognized as the heir.   8
Therefore there must be no return to the Elements (that
is the unseen powers which constitute the demonic character of the Law). He must remain in the freedom he has
now attained as the adopted son of God, and give up
worrying about special observances as if they were necessary to salvation. What the Galatians should try to do is   12
to imitate Paul, and retain their love for him. Where has
their personal attachment to him gone?

After this emotional parenthesis Paul returns to the   21
contrast between Law and Gospel and gives his famous
allegory of the two sons and two wives of Abraham. Hagar
was a slave, representing the Law, and her son was born

in bondage. Christians are the descendants not of Hagar but of Sarah, the free woman, and are consequently the children of freedom while the Jews, the spiritual descendants of Hagar, are in bondage.

v   In chapter v he begins to ask what freedom means. Here you have a clear choice, the Law or Christ. Circumcision involves obedience to the Law and if you accept it,

4   then you are in bondage to the whole Law. That implies severance from Christ and from the whole sphere of grace. But righteousness can be ours only through the free gift of the Spirit by the operation of faith. If we are in Christ circumcision cannot profit at all. The only thing of im-

7   portance is the faith that works through love. You were doing so well along this line. Why have you changed? You must know that this is my original teaching. Other-

13   wise why should I be persecuted? Freedom must be recognized not as licence to do what you like but as an opportunity to allow the Spirit to guide your conduct. You must allow the Spirit to take possession of you and to act in your every thought and word and deed. Under the influence of the Spirit we enjoy a rich personal freedom and are untrammelled by the need to obey the cramping regulations of the Law. Nevertheless by yielding to the Spirit's influence we actually fulfil the moral ideals of the

19   Law. Thus we are dead to all the enticements of sensuality and live lives worthy of the Kingdom of God.

vi   Paul concludes with a number of practical hints. 'You

6   are to deal gently with each other; especially look after your teachers and see that they are properly paid. There is to be no niggardliness; we reap only in proportion as

11   we sow.' He adds a personal postscript in his own writing. The Judaizers are a cowardly and bombastic lot of people,

only hoping to avoid persecution. But *our* one boast is that we have already been crucified with Christ. The important thing is that we should begin life all over again, and we can be created anew if we submit ourselves to the Spirit. He prays for the peace of the 'New' Israel, thus putting on one side the present representatives of the Jewish nation and claiming for the Christian Church the title of Israel as heir to the promises of the Scriptures, the New Israel in contrast to the old. These people, he says, boast about their circumcision, but I have scars too and the best scars are not those inflicted by the surgeon's knife, but those won in the service of Christ.

This concludes the epistles written during the Second Journey.

CHAPTER III

Letters of the Third Journey

A YEAR after his return to Antioch Paul was out on his travels again for the Third Journey. He halted at Ephesus for more than two years, preaching in the school of Tyrannus. Early in that stay he heard disquieting news from Corinth. It was there, we remember, that he had worked for eighteen months on his second journey, and there that he had written his two letters to the Thessalonians.

Corinth was interesting from many points of view. The most important city in Greece and capital of the Roman province, it was situated on the narrow ridge of land between two Gulfs. In our time a canal has been cut through, making a passage from one gulf to the other, but that canal was not there in St. Paul's time. Nero tried to make one a little later in 66, but the attempt was abandoned. At this time the city still dominated the two unjoined arms of the sea.

Corinth was thoroughly cosmopolitan and highly immoral. Paul and his friends had converted there a few Jews and a considerable number of Gentiles during the Second Journey. Among the Jews was Crispus, ruler of the synagogue, while among the Gentiles there was Justus, a Roman proselyte, with whom he stayed. During St. Paul's residence Gallio became Proconsul, and when the Jews, outraged by the Apostle's teaching, dragged Justus before his court, Gallio refused to hear the case, thus in

36

effect giving judgement in his favour. Paul did not stay long after that but left with Aquila and Priscilla to keep the Passover in Jerusalem. This done, he returned for a short stay in Antioch, where he wrote 'Galatians'. Then he started off again on his third journey, and here he is at Ephesus receiving news from Corinth. He hears of grave cases of immorality which had occurred among the Christian converts there, and he starts a correspondence with them, which on his side really consists of four letters. Their main object is to establish his personal leadership and to assert his own authority in order to bring his converts back to the sincerity of the gospel and its way of life. He had much the same sort of object in view as in writing to the Galatians but the subjects treated are entirely different.

The first letter remains to us only in a fragmentary form. It consists of 2 Corinthians vi. 14 to vii. 1. In it Paul deals directly with the moral question. It is possible that the difficulty had arisen as a result of the Christians' attendance at pagan banquets. These festivities were associated with idol worship and only too often that worship was mixed up with immorality. If the converts had been attending the social gatherings they may have found temptation too strong for them, with the consequence that their moral tone was in danger of being lowered to that of their environment.

Paul tells them not to mix with unbelievers. There is no contact between Christ and the devil, between the temple of God and idols. He drives that lesson home with a quotation from 'Isaiah', a manifesto of the post-exilic period demanding that Jews should keep themselves en- *vi* 14

tirely to themselves and not be contaminated by contact
with the heathen.

> 'Touch not, my People, aught that is not clean
> And I will then receive you as my own,
> And be a Father to you, saith your God,
> While you shall sons and daughters be to me.'

These promises, says St. Paul, now apply to the New Israel.
Let us therefore perfect our holiness, and keep free from
every defilement of soul and body. Then God will indeed
show Himself our Father.

That is the only fragment of the first letter which we
have left. Whether it made much difference in the attitude
of the readers is not clear. However, soon after receiving
it the Corinthians wrote to Paul, and they must have been
affected to some extent by what he said because they ask
his advice about certain questions such as marriage and
celibacy, meats offered to idols, the proper rights and
privileges of an apostle, the Sacraments—particularly the
correct method of celebrating the Lord's Supper, spiritual
gifts, and the doctrine of the Resurrection. At the same
time Paul heard also from Chloe, who lived in Corinth
and had a small body of Christians meeting in her house.
She tells him there is a good deal of party strife, various
sections of the community rallying round different leaders.
Also there is reported a grave case of incest.

Paul dealt with these subjects in his second letter to the
Corinthians, which we know to-day as 1 Corinthians. He
sent it by the short sea route and at the same time he sent
Timothy round by the land route, to go as his personal

representative in order to bring the Corinthians to a better frame of mind.

I CORINTHIANS—*Many questions*

After giving his usual salutation and thanksgiving Paul *i* embarks on a series of warnings about the evil of party 10 spirit. He thinks it is lucky that he did not baptize anybody himself except Crispus and Gaius and the household of Stephanas. He cannot therefore be properly charged with 18 forming a party. He tries to recall the simplicity of the cross, which is the centre of the whole plan of salvation. That simplicity stands in complete contrast both to Jewish pedantry and to Hellenic philosophy. By it God has stulti- 26 fied worldly wisdom.

He says that he teaches only Jesus and His cross. He *ii* does not deal in the esoteric wisdom of this world. It is one of the common themes of St. Paul that plain simple facts should be enough for any of us. We should avoid all 6 tedious and pseudo-scientific explanations. Here he is really aiming his attack against the beginning of the sort of theosophy which later became known as Gnosticism, the supreme example of the false application of science to religion. This foolish wisdom of the world is contrasted with the true wisdom of the spirit; but this latter wisdom 14 is only discernible by the regenerate, because he alone possesses the Holy Spirit.

Unfortunately the Corinthians are still earthbound. *iii* Paul cannot lead them on to higher flights as he would like to do. He is bound to keep them to the easiest things— they are only babes and must be fed with milk. That is 3

why he must again begin to try to make the followers of
10 the different parties realize their foolishness. 'You are
merely', he says, 'sections of one structure; I laid the
foundations, what does it matter if someone else raises
another story on those foundations. You cannot really
oppose the builders to each other; you must take our work
as one whole.' 'In any case', he adds, 'everything is tested.
16 You are the temple of God which we are engaged in
building, but look upon your privileged position in
humility and do not boast of your knowledge. Try not to
be superior.'

iv   He asks them with some irony not to pass any premature
5   judgement on him. No doubt they are important people.
He himself is just one of the world's cast-offs. They can
keep their importance if they like and leave him his
humility, but they will soon see where the true religion
14 really lies. He adds, 'Timothy is visiting you, do let him
find you following the example I first taught you. Later
on I shall come myself. Am I to come in gentleness or
with a big stick? It is for you to say.'

v   Next, having dealt with party spirit he discusses church
discipline. It is a grave question. There is this charge of
incest. The offender must be removed, and the same
applies to all evil-living people. They must be eliminated
7   as completely as old leaven before the Passover. 'You
must get them right out of the system of the body politic
9   or there can be no progress in the Christian life. My last
letter warned you against evil contacts. What I mean is
that you must boycott any of our own people convicted
of gross evil.'

vi   Litigation on such or other matters must not be taken
to a pagan court. We must deal with our own brethren

ourselves. It is better to suffer injury than to engage in secular lawsuits with one another. You must not try to justify licentiousness on the ground that Christians are free and can do anything they like. Sexual connexion implies psychological relationship. Therefore it is an insult to Christ Himself if you have illicit sexual relations, because you are already united with Him. Paul believed quite firmly that people who are thus associated participate in each other's personality. He believed that the physical act has its reactions in the psychological, and even in the metaphysical, spheres. We have been made one with Christ, therefore we must not prostitute our bodies. 12

Paul then gets down to the questions asked. The first is that of marriage and celibacy. Marriage is to be honoured and its physical obligations must be fulfilled. You must behave in accordance with the proper obligations of the condition in which you find yourself. But each must be certain of his own vocation. There must be no divorce. You must remain faithful even if you find yourself united to a pagan spouse. But if the pagan spouse wishes to break the marriage then you must let him or her loose. In such a case you are free to marry again. (That is what is known to canonists as 'the Pauline privilege', and it has entered into many arguments about the nature of married life and the possibility of divorce.) With regard to the advisability of marriage, Paul says, if you take my advice you won't seek to change your condition whatever it is. The same applies to people who have been circumcised—stay in the condition in which you are. Again, if you are a slave, do not try to get your freedom. But if you are free do not become any man's slave. The same advice applies to virgins and widows, unless indeed they find the desire to *vii*

8

17

21

25

marry exceptionally strong. The Second Coming is imminent and there is not much time. Therefore remain as
you are.

It is extraordinary that in the first burst of a great
religious enthusiasm St. Paul's teaching on this subject
should be so moderate and so full of common sense. Anybody of experience can recognize here the advice of one
who really does understand human psychology and is not
swept away by fanaticism into forgetting its common limi-
tations. It would have been well if all religious teachers
could have retained so calm a balance.

viii   The second question relates to the permissibility of eating meat offered to idols. The reply is that the inquirers
must not be too 'knowing'. What they have to remember
4   is that love should be the basis of all conduct. Idols are
really nothing, but if you knowingly eat meat that has been
offered to them you are flouting the conscience of the man
7   who is inclined to be scrupulous. We must show consideration to such people, and it is better to be a plain vegetarian
than to be a stumbling-block in another's path.

ix   He deals next with the rights of an apostle. The question arose out of the fact that St. Paul, unlike most of the
missionary leaders, had not demanded hospitality from
those whom he evangelized. Did his failure to do so show
4   some doubt about his standing? There is no doubt, he
affirms, about his status as an apostle. He therefore enjoyed
all the usual privileges of an apostle in regard to food, in
respect of the capacity to marry, and in the right to receive
free board and lodging. Why then did he not demand his
15   keep? The answer is, simply because he wanted to preach
without any charge, so that he might be able to say he had
proclaimed the Gospel without accepting a penny for it.

He makes himself a slave to everybody. He continually 19
exercises himself to make sure of his own success in the
race of life. He does not accept any luxuries but keeps his 23
body in subjection so that he can run his race successfully.

The following chapter deals with the sacraments, Jewish, *x*
Christian and pagan. Baptism was prefigured in the
Red Sea and in the cloud of the desert wanderings. The
Eucharist was foretold in the story of the Rolling Rock.
(Here Paul alludes to the Rabbinic legend that the rock
which Moses struck rolled along and followed the Israelites
during their journeyings to give them continual drink in
the wilderness.) The pagans also have their rites but you 6
must not share in them because they generally lead to
immorality and so incur God's wrath, as indeed happened
with the Jews. But God will not let you be tempted above
your capacity to resist. You must keep to your own sacred 14
meal, in which you share in the Body and Blood of Christ;
and so cement your union with one another in Him. Jews, 18
Christians and pagans have each their own altars, but you
cannot share in them all. The food offered at pagan altars
is offered to demons and you cannot share both with the
Lord and with demons. Stick to your own worship, but 25
don't be over-scrupulous about food. If the doubt arises
whether any meat you are eating has been sacrificed to
idols do not ask unnecessary questions. Eat what is put
before you and do not go out of your way to discover a
difficulty. If you cannot escape the question you will have
to decide it and you will have to think about the other
person's conscience, but it is much better left to ignorance.
Don't press your freedom in such matters so far as to make 29
others stumble.

The next question is that of public worship. Women *xi*

must always have their heads covered in time of service but men must remove their head-dress. (This was contrary to the Jewish custom, according to which men still remain covered.) 'Do not spoil your worship by letting party dis-

20 cussions get into your churches. That has led to your mistake about the Lord's Supper. The way you are doing it now is quite wrong. You are making it into a convivial meal; it is not meant to be a meal but a token repast. It is a religious ceremony with traditional words and actions

27 attached to it by the Lord's own authority. Our spiritual health depends in large measure upon the way in which we use this essentially Christian rite. Therefore we must exercise special care in our approach to it.'

xii Paul then speaks about spiritual gifts. He says pagans and Christians alike are subject to supernatural influences. But the Christian's Spirit is evidenced in his confession of

7 Christ, and it is manifested in a variety of gifts. Each be-

12 liever has his own characteristic gift. 'You are the body of Christ and each individual limb has its own function.'

xiii The best gift of all is *agapē*, love. In the thirteenth chapter Paul gives his famous 'Hymn to Love' with its description

xiv and analysis of this fundamental virtue. Then in the fourteenth he goes on, 'If you want to know what is the second best gift, it is prophecy. This is far better than what you are running after, the gift of tongues, which

7 many of you have and use frequently in your worship. Such a habit of speaking in ecstasy is no doubt showy, but it is unintelligible. It is not really so good as prophecy or preaching, which other people can understand and by

12 which they can profit. Do therefore try to cultivate the

26 gift of prophecy. Above all preserve order in your public

34 worship. Let each one take his part according to his gift,

but only one at a time.   Women have no rights in this
matter: their business is to preserve silence in church.

   In chapter xv he deals with the Resurrection. He begins   *xv*
with a record of the appearances of the risen Christ,
reckoning the vision vouchsafed to himself as the last, and
then goes on to point out how our rising again is bound up   12
in His. The two are indissolubly connected and that is
the basis of the whole Christian faith. When Christ appears   20
again there will be a general resurrection, which will be
followed by the end of the world and the coming of the
Kingdom, and will include the destruction of every
demonic power, so that God will be all in all. That is the
Christian belief. That indeed is the only belief that can   29
justify the practice of baptism for the dead. (Apparently
there were those who were so anxious to have their whole
family together in the Resurrection, and for that reason to
have them all included within the society of the Christian
Church, that they were actually having themselves baptized as proxies on behalf of those who had died without
receiving the Sacrament.) That belief, says Paul, is also
the only justification for his own daily death in suffering
and self-denial. He goes on to a discussion of the nature of   35
the Resurrection body. It will not have the same characteristics as the body we possess now. It will be a different
body, as fruit is different from the seed that gave it birth;
but the identity of the individual will be preserved in spite
of the change. The body of anyone who is still alive at the
Second Coming will be transformed at the final trumpet
call. We shall then acquire a new instrument for our
personality which will be nevertheless a proper successor
to the present body and will be actually linked in definite
continuity with it, just as the new grain is the natural

42   result of the death and burial of the seed corn. The new
      body will be infinitely more glorious than the old, and it
45   will be immortal. The former will share in the nature of
      Christ's body as the latter shared in the nature of Adam's.
      He concludes that this will be the final victory of life over
54   death. In the meantime we must continue faithful in our
      work, knowing that since it is linked with Christ's it will
      certainly come to fruition.

          That finishes the doctrinal part of the Epistle; but Paul
xvi   ends with a personal note about the collection for the
      saints in Jerusalem, and promises that he will visit his
5   readers after he has completed his tour of Macedonia.
10   They are to give all possible help to Timothy—Apollos
      may come later. He adds his greetings and signature in
22   his own hand, with a postscript urging them once more to
      avoid contact with those who have no love for Christ.

          Unfortunately this letter failed to have the desired effect
      in restoring the situation in Corinth, as did also Timothy's
      visit; so Paul went himself to try to get things straight.
      To his surprise he was very badly received, in fact so badly
      that he turned his back on the city and returned to Ephesus.
      From there he wrote to them his third, what he calls his
      'severe' letter, 2 Corinthians x to xiii. That letter was
      carried to Corinth by Titus, who was older and more ex-
      perienced than Timothy, and consequently might be
      expected to have more influence with the recalcitrants.
      In it Paul answers certain charges that had been brought
      against him.

2 CORINTHIANS x–xiii—*Answer to Charges*

The first charge is that of feebleness. It is alleged that *x* the high tone adopted in his letters is not sustained when he is physically present. Paul says his weapons are not those of flesh and blood, nor does he put on airs, but he is at least as good as his letters. He is prepared to punish any insubordination. It is no good saying that he appears a 7 person of importance only when he puts pen to paper. His presence, however feeble it may be, is just as formid- able as his epistles. He goes on in a more affectionate tone, 14 'After all you are my own people; you were given me by God and I am your original missionary. I am sure that you will yet come up to the proper pattern of behaviour. Thus you will encourage me to press on with the work of evangelization in regions hitherto untouched.'

The second charge is his refusal of hospitality. 'I am *xi* very fond of you and I do hope you will not forsake me for those other so-called apostles who are trying to entice you away from me. Though I realize that I am not much of a speaker, yet I do know my subject. In spite of that I do 7 not want your financial help. I want to follow my trade and live at my own charges. You must not hold this against me, as I am doing it merely in order to put to shame the false apostles who give themselves such airs but who will surely come to a bad end.'

The third charge is that of defective authority. 'I find 16 I must blow my own trumpet in order to compete with other claimants on your attention. If you look into my race and descent as well as into the records of my sufferings for the cause, you will see that I am in every respect pre- ferable to those people after whom you are beginning to run so unwisely.' This section gives an imposing summary of Paul's qualifications and adventures, including an eloquent plea for understanding of the emotional strain under which he suffers.

xii   The fourth charge is the lack of spiritual experience. It is all very well, Paul suggests, for them to put such tremendous emphasis upon the kind of ecstasy with which he had dealt in his last letter. Actually he has himself enjoyed more privileges in that respect than others. 'I had one particular experience of ecstasy fourteen years ago, whose precise nature I have never been able to define but which brought with it a supreme revelation of the inner mysteries of life and salvation. That kind of thing is not infrequent with me. The very illness that you have observed in me is as a matter of fact a corrective that God has given me

11   so that I shall not be carried away by such transports. In spite of that weakness my powers of working miracles are not exceeded by any of those super-apostles of yours. I have given you the benefit of all this and have only denied you the pleasure of entertaining me.'

14   The fifth charge is the question of support. 'I am quite determined that on my third visit, when I do come to see you again, I will not be a burden to you. I will not accept financial support. It is no good suggesting that this is

16   some trick on my part to get behind your defences. You will have found that Titus adopts the same attitude as I

19   do. Are we, you and I, really going to disappoint one another? Do not let me be humiliated by your lack of penitence for the really deplorable conduct of which some of you have been guilty.'

xiii   Then follows a final appeal and warning. 'My third

5   visit,' he says, 'will be a very serious occasion. It will be

a visit for discipline; therefore examine yourselves carefully in preparation for it. If you do that you may avoid
a summary judgement when I come.'

After despatching this letter Paul resumed his third
missionary journey and travelled in Macedonia. While
thus engaged he was met by Titus, who brought the good
news that by a majority vote the Corinthians had condemned the person who had flouted Paul's authority. On
the receipt of this report he immediately wrote his fourth
letter, which is 2 Corinthians i–ix (omitting vi. 14 to vii. 1).
He forgives his opponents, and takes the opportunity to
say what a grand and glorious thing the Christian ministry
is.

2 CORINTHIANS i–ix—*Reconciliation*

In the introduction Paul speaks of the way in which he *i*.3
had suffered over this controversy; how he has now been
comforted, and how he hopes in turn to comfort his
readers. From the depth of despair he has been lifted to 8
the height of thanksgiving. He vindicates his recent
actions. His behaviour has been sincere. He has twice 12
tried to visit them and did fully intend to do so. His 15
failure does not imply fickleness: he is as constant as
Christ in whom they all live. The change of plan was only
in order to spare them embarrassment. He did not wish *ii*
to come to them a second time in painful circumstances.
He reiterates the point of the last letter. It was written in 4
tears, not in order to pain them but to let them understand
how much love he bore them. Now the man who caused

the trouble has been condemned, and so they can all forgive and forget. He had to test their obedience, but now he is prepared fully to endorse their formal pardon if they give it. Indeed he has actually anticipated their

12 action and himself pardoned the offender. Whatever has happened at Corinth, elsewhere his work has been one triumphal progress. May they all prove big enough for the task God has given them.

iii This leads to a discourse on the splendour of the ministry. We know each other very well, he says, and we need no further mutual commendation. How great the Christian

4 ministry is! It is even greater than that of the old dispensation. We all realize how wonderful the ministry of Moses was because of the radiance that shone from his face. But his ministry was of the Law, a matter of regulations and punishments. If that was glorious, surely a ministry of acquittal must be more glorious. And whereas Moses' ministry was only a transient one our Christian ministry

12 is permanent. What is its special glory? It is the simplicity and sincerity of its message. The candour of the Gospel has removed the veil that Moses had to wear, and the glory thus made visible is so great and intense that it actually changes into its own nature those on whom it shines.

iv The light of the Gospel frees the ministry from any

3 suspicion of duplicity. Only evil can blind us to its truth and value. But God gives us a practical experience of life as a result of which His glory can be seen reflected in the face of Christ. Even our suffering serves to reveal Him

7 more clearly. Our ministry is no doubt weak and inefficient, yet it represents so clear a call from God that we

12 are actually bound to speak. The conviction is so strong

within us that it must be proclaimed. We tell it to others in order that they may be brought to share in that triumph which belongs to Christ and all who serve Him. In spite 16 of all weakness we can still continue the good work. As our physical powers decline, so our spiritual powers grow until we emerge into that life which is eternal. We are *v* strengthened by the certain knowledge that the earthly will be succeeded by the heavenly, towards which we all press forward as to a goal, God all the time preparing us for the new conditions in which we shall live. My ministry 11 is one of reconciliation. My business is to reconcile people to Christ. I wish to give you some justification for supporting me against those who think me a bit mad. Our outlook is increasingly spiritual. I no longer recognize people, even Christ Himself, by their physical attributes. We are in point of fact a new creation in Christ. 'A new creation'; that is what our changed relation to God really means. Our ministry brings others into the sphere of that reconciliation in which we are all new-made. As an envoy of 20 Christ I make a direct appeal. I beg you, make your peace with God. Seize the opportunity to-day, do not put it off. *vi* The result of my sufferings has been to make my ministry more effective. I know I am talking too much, but 11 you should reciprocate and give your confidence to me.[1]

Give me a place in your affections. You know I am very *vii*.2 proud of you. I cannot tell you how glad I am that the 5 crisis is settled. My relief at your reception of Titus was very great. I am afraid my letter upset you, but I recognize that the grief you felt was of the right kind; it did bring you to a proper frame of mind. My severity was intended 12

[1] For vi. 14–vii. 1 see pp. 37–38 above.

to give you an opportunity to show your regard for me; and the result has delighted Titus and vindicated everything I said.

viii   With the next section Paul gets into his practical mood again. He strikes a note of urgency, and gives as the reason the importance of justifying the confidence he has placed in them. They can do this by subscribing to the collection for the poor saints in Jerusalem. Titus, who launched the

9   scheme, is relying on them. Let them think of the Lord's generosity, and remember that all should try to help one another and so equalize their burdens. They can be sure

16   of the agents in this act of charity. He gives a personal guarantee of the *bona fides* of Titus and of the two others who were assisting in the collection, probably Luke and Apollos.

ix   He assures them that he is confident of a liberal response, seeing that they have justified all the things he has said in boasting about their preparations. Let everything be got ready beforehand and let men see in their generosity a proof that Christians practise what they preach.[1]

Paul followed up this letter with a personal appearance at Corinth. He had intended to extend this third missionary journey to include a visit to Rome, but the business of the collection went ahead so well that he began to realize it was important that he himself should go with those who were taking the money to Jerusalem. The new plan broke into his intention to go to Rome. Before leaving Corinth he therefore wrote to the imperial capital to tell the Christians there how sorry he was not to be able to visit them on this occasion. However, his intention after deliver-

[1] For chapters x–xiii see pp. 47–49 above.

ing the money is to visit Spain, and when he goes there he will take the opportunity of calling in at Rome. This letter, which is typical in its casual origin, turns out to be the most important of all the Pauline Epistles.

There is a change of method. The writer enjoys a new ease of mind as a result of the successful termination of the Corinthian incident, and that leads him into a larger treatment. He is not dealing with personal questions, because he has never been to Rome. He is therefore able to look out on a wider horizon and to give a fuller exposition of his fundamental teaching than in the earlier Epistles. What we have in the Epistle to the Romans is nothing less than a philosophy of history and a theology of salvation.

In Rome there was a big colony of Jews and there were many synagogues. The Jews were not popular: nevertheless they had won a considerable number of proselytes. Apparently the arrival of Christianity in their midst caused some rioting. There had been trouble in 51 or 52 when the Jews were driven out of Rome by Claudius. They were expelled, says Suetonius, because of riots which occurred at the instigation of somebody called Chrestus. It looks as though the historian does not know the proper spelling of the name Christ, but is at least aware that Christians had been mixed up in the affair. How had Christianity arrived at Rome? In all probability the Church was founded there as a result of the ordinary traffic between the capital and the eastern part of the empire. There had been no great individual apostle to found a church. Aquila and Priscilla, we know, had come from Rome, but it is certain that as yet no distinguished missionary had been there, because Paul says he will never build on another man's foundation. In later years Rome

was always able to boast of a double apostolic foundation
by Peter and Paul. This is quite well attested in the next
century, and it suggests that both were there after the date
of this letter. However, that is beside the present point.
The probability is that originally a number of Christians
had come from the East and settled down in Rome. They
had begun to have dealings with the proselytes and with
the congregations of the synagogues. From those sources
a Christian community had been gradually built up.
It is to that particular group that St. Paul wrote this
letter.

ROMANS, A.D. 56–*Faith and the Law*

i   Paul begins with the usual sort of opening in which he
8   introduces himself, explains his mission, and thanks God
18   for the Christian loyalty of his readers. He then strikes one
of the dominant notes of the Epistle, the certainty of judgement. Judgement, he says, has been declared on the
Gentile world because it fails to discern the witness God
has given of Himself in nature and so is powerless to
24   produce a good life. Sexual perversion is rife throughout
pagan society, and it leads to psychological degeneracy.
ii   But if judgement has been pronounced on the pagan world
12   it has also been pronounced on the Jews. They will be
judged by their failure to live up to the Mosaic Law just
17   as the pagan is judged by his failure to attain the standard
of natural law. The Jews have not lived up to the moral
25   demands of their Law. Circumcision is of no value apart
from real goodness. Thus we can say that Gentile and Jew
have alike failed, for they have both missed the mark of

the opportunity offered them by their respective circumstances.

So we must conclude that sin is universal. Although the *iii*
Jew has the advantage of being the first medium of God's
self-revelation, God can still be angry with him. This
argues no inconsistency on the part of God. He is still just.   9
He shows no special favour to Jews. The fact is that no
one can be acquitted under the Law.

Then Paul begins to discuss the means of escape from this   21
appalling situation in which the whole world lies under
the condemnation of sin. The next few chapters deal with
this question on the psychological level. The main con-
tention is that we can escape only if we identify ourselves
by faith with Jesus. That is the one means of escape. If
we do that we are acquitted, if we do not we are not
acquitted, but are under condemnation still. That means   27
of course that there is no room for pride. You cannot earn
your salvation: you simply accept it as a free gift. The
Law was really intended to make this clear.   31

He takes the example of Abraham. Abraham's stand-   *iv*
ing with God was the reward, not of his circumcision, but
of his faith. His faith was noted *before* he was circumcised.
Similarly whatever was promised through Abraham to   9
posterity was precisely a promise, a free gift. It conferred   13
salvation upon his descendants on the same basis of faith,
that is trustful acceptance. You can see how that principle
is made clear in Abraham's own life. He staked every-   17
thing on his faith. He was quite incapable of producing
a child, and yet had faith to believe that even his impotence
would be overruled by divine providence, so that he could
have descendants. This confidence has its equivalent in   23
our faith in our risen Lord. The Christian's faith in Christ

risen is precisely the same psychologically as Abraham's acceptance of the promise of a child when he was past the age for procreation.

v   This principle is corroborated in the glorious confidence of the redeemed. Their afflictions test and reinforce that confidence. They have felt themselves acquitted by Christ's death and realize the great love thus shown for sinners. Accordingly they have all the stronger guarantee of ultimate salvation.

12   No doubt there was sin before the Law was given, and sin had as its consequence death. We know that both the sin and the death arose from the transgression of the one
15   man, the original Adam. The free gift of eternal life from God also comes by one Man, the second Adam, but it differs from the Law in bringing not death but life, and it releases from the damage done by many sins and not
20   merely from that done by one sin. If you want to know what part the Law played in the whole of this history, the answer is that the purpose of the Law was to underline the heinousness of sin. Men might have glossed over sin, if it had not been for the Law. When once its true motive was made clear, grace took possession. Law was no longer supreme, but God's promise and God's free gift took the place of the whole legal system.

vi   In Christ there is therefore a definite transition from death to life. That is what is implied in Baptism. Beneath the water you appear to die; when you are raised out of
8   it you come once more to life. Being dead to sin we are
15   alive to God. We must conduct ourselves accordingly. This does not mean that because we are no longer under law we have freedom to sin, but that we are now wholly committed to the life of holiness. Henceforth we are slaves

not to the bad but to the good. We have changed the
whole character of our existence. Whereas sin was natural
to us before, holiness is natural to us now. We find a   20
fervent joy in the new circumstances. And this state issues
in eternal life.

The union with Christ which is the basis of the new life   *vii*
means freedom from law. Just as a widow is free from the
law of marriage because her husband is dead, so the
Christian is free from Law and sin, because as far as they
are concerned he is dead and he is now free of his obligations to them. For him Law has been brought to an end   4
by his death to the world and his rising again to a new life.
The actual function of the Law has been fulfilled in reveal-   7
ing the carnality of our nature. This does not mean that   13
the Law itself is evil. It has indeed awakened the dormant
sense of sin. It has shown me that I can do no good of
myself. It has made me continually conscious of a war
in myself, mind against body, Law against transgression.
What power can release me from this devastating conflict?   24
Thank God, He will Himself do it through Jesus Christ
our Lord.

We are then sure of the ultimate glory. There is no   *viii*
condemnation for those who are in Christ. In our flesh
He has won the victory over sin. There is no condemnation for us because in Him our nature has been changed.
We are no longer carnal but spiritual, for we have received
the spirit of divine sonship. Our present sufferings are   18
quite small compared with the future glory that shall be
ours. Hope is now the characteristic virtue of our life, a
force driving us on to grasp the future and achieve it. The   26
Spirit stirs up our good desires and our prayers. He is a
creative force within us, and makes everything turn out

31 for our good. If God is for us none can be against us. We are winning an overwhelming victory.

ix Having thus completed the psychological part of his argument Paul begins to deal with the historical aspect. He treats first the rejection of the Jews. He is very troubled because the Jews for the time being appear to have lost their place in God's plan. They are his people and he feels for them. He would be quite willing to lose the chance of salvation himself if he could thereby save his fellow-
6 countrymen. After all they were given the promise, and if God is stable and true, as he believes, then the promise must be secure. The fact is that not all Jews belong to the
10 true Israel. This may be seen from the history of Isaac, himself the child of promise. It was only to his line and not to that of his brother Ishmael that the promise was
14 made. Again Jacob was preferred to Esau. Can God choose whom He likes? Certainly. God is a supreme sovereign and no one has any right to challenge His choice. His prerogative is to set aside some and accept others. It looks as if for the time being the Jews are rejected. In
30 point of fact what has happened is that they have tripped up. They have encountered a stumbling block in the emphasis they have laid on works as against faith. They think that salvation must be earned.

x Therefore we see them rejected because they want to establish a righteousness of their own. But, as we have
9 seen, our only hope is in Jesus our Lord. We are safe if we confess Him with heart and mind. He is the one salva-
16 tion for Greek and Jew alike, and everyone alike must have the chance of hearing the good news. As it is, Israel
xi is the one nation which has rejected the gospel. That rejection, however, is only partial and temporary. There

is always a faithful remnant, a small body in whom the truth is found. In point of fact for those who are elect of God the free gift is still there. Through the lapse of those who rejected it salvation has come to the pagans, and they are offered it in order that others may be encouraged to emulate them in accepting it as a free gift. But the pagans 13 must not boast. Do not think this is a special favour given you in order that you can look down in superiority on other people. You are only grafted twigs; and the roots of the tree still remain in the old soil. God will be as stern 19 with you as with the Jews. If you really understand this mystery, this revealed secret, then that will stop all your 25 tendency to boast. You will realize that you get your chance only through the temporary defection of the Jews. When your number is made up the Jews will get their chance again. How inscrutable are God's ways! His is the 30 universe and one day it will all return to Him.

Do not then be superior; each limb has a place in the *xii* body. Fulfil each your own function according to your 3 own gift. You must be loving and helpful to everybody, full of enthusiasm, and careful to overcome evil with good. 8

This concludes the doctrinal part of the letter. Paul now turns to practical matters.

He deals first with the present crisis. It demands the *xiii* most careful conduct. You do not want any further 3 trouble with the government, therefore you must be particularly careful to submit to authority. Be honest in 5 every respect, and so avoid undesirable contacts with the 8 police. Pay your taxes promptly, owe no debt except that of love. The day is breaking: put off all deeds of darkness and live in the light.

You are in a mixed society, therefore respect others' *xiv*

5   scruples, especially at table. Do not criticize each other,
     particularly when there is a question of special observances.
13   Everything must be done to the glory of God. Remember
     that the Kingdom of God is peace and joy in the Holy
     Ghost, not eating and drinking. It is only when you begin
19   to succumb to doubts that things become unclean. Behave
     so that others may act always without doubtfulness and in
     a good conscience.

xv   Live together in common happiness. Try to please your
4   neighbour so as to do him good. God grant you mutual
     harmony. Show a cordial hospitality to one another as
7   Jesus did to both pagan and Jew.

14   Paul then refers to his impending visit. He has taken
17   his courage in both hands in reminding them of his com-
     mission from God as an Apostle to the Gentiles. Marvellous
     success has attended his work in preaching right from
     Jerusalem to Illyria. He has no wish to build on another
20   man's foundation. But now he hopes to come to them on
     his way to Spain. At the moment, however, he is on his
     way to Jerusalem to take the alms offered by the churches
25   in Macedonia. When he has completed that business he
     will set out for Spain and will call at Rome on the way.
     In the meantime he calls for their prayers, particularly for
     the success of his charitable mission to Jerusalem.

xvi The Epistle ends with a surprisingly long list of greetings
17   to individual Christians in Rome, and with a solemn warn-
     ing not to listen to any tale-bearing, however plausible,
     whose only effect will be to cause scandal and divisions.

CHAPTER IV

Letters from Prison

AFTER he had written the Epistle to the Romans, Paul went on, with the alms he had collected, to Jerusalem, and in due course delivered them. Through the animosity of the Jews he was arrested, and was forced to make his appeal to Cæsar. This ultimately brought him to Rome in very different circumstances from those he had fore-shadowed. Imprisoned in the imperial city, he kept in touch with affairs while he was under examination. News was brought to him of the churches in Asia and especially of that at Colosse. Paul himself had not been responsible for building up the Christian community in that particular town. Its foundation was due to his friend Epaphras. The Colossians, he was told, were doing well but it appeared that they were in danger from a new kind of teaching, possibly a sort of Christian Essenism. It looks as if the Jewish Essenes had taken on a certain amount of Christian teaching and combined it with some form of esoteric 'wisdom'. They practised circumcision, not as necessary to salvation, but as a help to perfection. And they had developed a cult of angels. It may have been an early example of that Gnosticism which was to be a serious menace to the Christian Church in later years.

St. Paul writes to the Colossians and tells them that salvation is to be found only in Christ. Jesus is the Head of the Church and they must stick to His teaching. He warns them against 'superior wisdom' and bids them live good moral lives in Christ.

This is a specially interesting letter because it is more detached than the earlier ones, even than Romans. Just because St. Paul did not know the Colossians it may have been easier for him to talk to them in general terms. Also this was a circular letter intended to be passed on to the Laodiceans. In the absence of local detail it was possible to deal with wider issues. Further, his imprisonment gave Paul an opportunity to think out his religious philosophy more clearly. This will become plain as we consider the contents of the epistle.

COLOSSIANS, A.D. 59– *The Universal Christ.*

i

9

15

After expressing his gratitude for the tremendous progress of the Gospel and praying for future advance he discusses the person of Christ and His work. He is getting into a different atmosphere from that in which the earlier letters were conceived. Christ, he says, was God's agent in creation, the creation not only of the material world but also of the supernatural. Paul is here describing Jesus not as a historic but as a cosmic Christ, not a Christ who belongs to a particular date or particular country but a Christ of the whole universe, the Father's firstborn and

18

the pre-existent Prince of the whole creation. As such, Christ is also the head of the divine body, the Church. In Him the full plenitude of Deity has its abode. Through the blood of His cross the universe has been reconciled to God, and a restoration of all things both in heaven and on

21

earth has been effected. 'As you are members of His body

you yourselves have now been reconciled to God and are free from every charge.' Paul says that he is glad of his 24 suffering on their behalf, for by it he is enabled to own a share in Christ's redemptive work. His duty is to proclaim the mystery of God's design, and to show that Christ is the appointed Messiah for both Jew and Gentile.

His present struggle is to help them (and the Laodiceans) ii to persevere. He goes on to give them a warning against error. Let them stick to the teaching they have received and avoid all foolish traditions about demonic beings. In Christ they are spiritually circumcised, and because that is so they are free from the Law; therefore they need not 16 worry about the regulations of the Law itself nor those finicking details about the cult of angels which people have spun out for themselves. They are dead to all such fancies 20 of so-called higher thought.

In point of fact they enjoy a new life in Christ. They are iii risen with Christ and therefore live in Him. Let the flesh 5 and its vices die. Cultivate, instead, the virtues of Christ, ignoring every barrier of race, class and culture. Live in 12 love and peace and in one grand sweet song.

This practical teaching he sums up in a moral code. (Most of the remaining Epistles finish with such a moral code. Paul probably took the example from the philosophers of the day who, in lecturing on ethics, would give a table of manners, showing people how they ought to behave in society. The codes as they are handled by St. Paul seem like lecturer's notes on appropriate conduct for various classes of people.)

Thus he details the right conduct for wives and hus- 18 bands, fathers and children, slaves and masters. In each iv case he suggests that being 'in the Lord' makes all the difference. Paganism can give a select list of virtues but not the power to attain them. But if you are in Christ you have all the moral strength needed to fulfil adequately the duties of your social status.

2   All alike must persevere in prayer, and especially should they pray for him that he may use to the full the opportunities presented even by his present unpromising condition for witnessing to Christ. They themselves must be careful how they approach non-Christians, and they must deal with each individual in the manner appropriate to his needs.

7   The Epistle ends with personal greetings and with instructions to the church of Colosse to exchange their letter with that addressed to Laodicea.

EPHESIANS, A.D. 59–60– *The Church—God's Secret*

The letter to the Colossians was not the only epistle carried by Tychicus and Onesimus from Paul, prisoner in Rome, to a church in Asia Minor. There was also one to Laodicea, a town about twelve miles to the west of Colosse. Some scholars, both ancient and modern, have judged it to be identical with our 'Ephesians'. Certainly the name Ephesus is omitted from the address of this epistle in certain important manuscripts. A favourite view at the present time is that 'Ephesians' is a circular letter meant to be read in a number of churches, including those of Laodicea and Hierapolis, and that the address was purposely left blank so that the appropriate name might be inserted by the reader of each congregation.

The very nature of such an 'encyclical' removes it from

the sphere of purely local controversy and makes a general treatment of common topics both possible and necessary. While the same ideas as had been dealt with in Colossians were still running in St. Paul's mind when he wrote this letter, he is here able to give a more positive and serene expression to his teaching. Especially with regard to the 'mystery' of God's purpose in history and the new life in the Church he reaches a joyous sublimity which is scarcely to be found elsewhere even in the New Testament. The renewed emphasis on a Moral Code for Christians should also be noticed.[1]

Ephesus was a place that Paul knew well. He had visited it on his second journey and it was there that he left Aquila and Priscilla. On his third journey he stayed there for a period of over two years, setting up a regular lecture room in the school of Tyrannus. His work was so successful and so many people were converted to Christianity that the idol-makers began to lose their trade. Paul only left the city when Demetrius, the silversmith, had tried to revive that trade by raising a tumult over the missionary's alleged attack on the local goddess Diana.

The letter begins with a discussion of God's secret purpose as now revealed. Christians, says St. Paul, were preselected in Christ by God in order that they might become the members of His family. It is to this family that God's secret has been made known. All history had been leading up to one great culminating moment when everything should be brought to a head in Christ. Of this movement the Jewish Christians were the first-fruits, but the pagans

i

3

7

11

---

[1] These two paragraphs are reprinted from Wand, *New Testament Letters* (O.U.P.), p. 112.

too have now yielded their quota to the Divine family and have received the gift of the Holy Spirit. This is a guarantee that one day all the elect shall be redeemed.

15   St. Paul prays that they may all have a fuller knowledge of God's intention in this historical movement. They must realize that the exalted power of Christ is applied universally through His headship of the family, the Church.

22   That Divine organization supplies a universal means of expression for the ascended Christ who is Himself a universal personality.

ii   The next section deals with sin and salvation. Paul reminds his readers that they too were once dead like Jesus, though not in any tomb of earth, but in the grave of

3   sin. So also were the Jews, but God has raised to a new life all those who are united with Christ, and He has done it not as a reward for any desert of theirs, but as a free

11   gift. The Gentiles too have been brought into this fellow-

13   ship by Christ. He has broken down the wall of partition which throughout the ages separated Jew from Gentile and was symbolized by the actual wall which in the Temple

17   divided the court of the Gentiles from that of Israel. Now Jew and Gentile, as they are found together in Christ, have equal rights of citizenship in the heavenly city.

iii   Next Paul discusses his own position as an exponent of

8   this great Divine mystery. He claims that it had been made known to him by a special revelation. But this plan of all the ages which has thus been made known to men is actually revealed through the Church not only to human beings but also to Rulers and Powers, that is the authorities of the spiritual world. Nothing, says Paul, can stop the spread of this revelation. He himself may be imprisoned and rendered apparently powerless, but the work

goes on. He prays that his readers may learn to grasp this   14
manifestation of God's love in all its fullness.

He then discusses the nature of the new life in the one   *iv*
Church. He instructs his readers carefully to maintain
that essential unity between Jew and Gentile of which they
have been apprised. As they are all members of one body,
so they share in one Spirit, one Lord, one faith, one
baptism, and one God and Father of all. This unity is   7
served by the ministerial gifts which were handed to His
people by the Lord on His Ascension. By such means the   14
individual will be able to grow to maturity through his
membership in the one Body. Therefore it is important   17
that each and all should abandon the old paganism with
all its characteristic vices.

Especially should they avoid all sexual impurity. This   *v*
he emphasizes by quoting the baptismal hymn: 3

> 'Awake O sleeper,
> From thy grave arise.
> The light of Christ upon thee shines.'

This refers to the familiar symbolism of baptism in which
the candidate for a moment appears to be drowned, dead
to all the old life, and immediately afterwards arises in the
full light of the sun to the new life in Christ. St. Paul goes   15
on to say that this new life should be full of that kind of
joy which naturally expresses itself in the music of their
antiphonal chanting.

Then, as before, he develops a moral code describing   22
the respective duties of wives and husbands, children and
fathers, slaves and masters. But this time there is a much   *vi*
stronger doctrinal background drawn from the life of the

10   Church. He finally charges his readers to put on the whole
armour of God, using each part of the infantryman's
equipment as symbolic of some special Christian gift.

PHILEMON

Another Epistle written about the same time is that to
Philemon. This is the only strictly personal letter of St.
Paul's that has come down to us. It is all about a runaway
slave, Onesimus, who was the actual bearer of the letter.
St. Paul is now returning him to his master, Philemon.
Onesimus has somehow encountered Paul in prison, and
there been converted to the Christian Faith. Paul thinks
that nothing can be quite right for him until he has re-
established his position with his master. The name
Onesimus means 'useful', and Paul hopes that Onesimus
will be as useful to Philemon in the future as he has already
proved to be to himself. Anyhow Onesimus is now acting
as postman and with Tychicus is carrying this letter, as
well as the two last, from Rome to the East.

The letter is too good to spoil by summary. It is earnest,
loving, playful and pastoral. Not even the best of the
longer letters reveals more clearly the endearing character
of Paul as pastor and friend.

PHILIPPIANS, A.D. 60–61–*Peace and Purity*

This was the last letter written during the imprisonment
at Rome, and if the Pastorals are not St. Paul's, it was
perhaps the last of all his letters.

Philippi, the town to which it was written, is in East Macedonia and was visited by St. Paul on his second journey. It was indeed the first town of Europe in which he established a church, and his special love for it lasted to the end. It was here that he had lodged with Lydia; healed the soothsayer; been flogged with Silas; and been delivered from prison by the frightened magistrates after an earthquake.

The church of Philippi consisted mostly of converts who had once been pagan. They were always ready with financial help, which St. Paul, contrary to his usual custom, gratefully accepted. There existed between the Apostle and these converts a mutual respect amounting to admiration. The only fault he had to find with them was that they were inclined to be a little jealous. The chief note of this letter is therefore one of joy and thanksgiving. But Paul still takes the opportunity to attack the Judaizers and the antinomians.

The optimistic strain comes out strongly in the first *i*
chapter, in which he thanks God for the good fellowship 3
he enjoys with the Philippians and goes on to pray for their 7
perfection. All is well, he says, with his missionary work. 12
His present plight has actually furthered it and has proved
no hindrance to the spread of the Gospel. He has no fears 19
for himself whether in life or in death; and he invites his
readers to lift up their hearts in defiance of their enemies. 27
The second chapter is a plea for peace and unity. The *ii*
Philippians should cultivate the humility shown by the
Son of God in His Incarnation. God is using them as His 12
instrument, they should therefore do everything without
complaint or argument. They will be cheered by the 19

knowledge that Timothy is coming to see them, and per-
25 haps later Paul will come himself. In the meantime
Epaphroditus, who had acted as their liaison officer with
Paul, is returning home to them after recovery from a grave
illness.

iii   Chapter iii begins the conclusion of the letter and deals
half apologetically with a well-worn topic. The readers
are to beware of Judaizers, the people who wish to bring
them under bondage to the Law. If anyone has a claim
7 to be a really good Jew it is surely Paul himself. But those
claims to Jewish eminence he is prepared to forfeit gladly
in order that he may experience instead the vitalizing
power of Christ. Thus united with Christ he is certain
that he will attain perfection and win the prize of Heaven.
15 They must learn to look at things in the same light.

17   They are also to beware of the antinomians, the people
who say that, because they have experienced the new
freedom, they need not obey any law. If anyone is tempted
to reason in that fashion, then he should remember to
imitate Paul himself and to avoid all false teachers whose
real aim is merely to escape the Cross and its suffering.
Christians must remember that they are in this world as
colonists from Heaven; their conduct must befit the
country from which they came and to which they will one
day return.

iv   There follows a little personal advice to Euodias and
Syntyche. They are told to drop their differences of
4 opinion and live at peace with one another. The rest are
advised not to be downhearted because of any apparent
8 setbacks, but to raise their spirits by continually dwelling
on fine thoughts.

10   For himself Paul is able to stand anything, but never-

theless he is grateful to them for their kind and generous help. He is quite overwhelmed by the gift they have sent him through Epaphroditus.

THE PASTORALS, A.D. 62–3, or A.D. 67–*Church Organization*

These letters are called Pastorals because they instruct Christian pastors how to look after their flock.

If they were actually written by St. Paul he must have been released from his imprisonment at Rome. He may then have gone to Spain and later resumed his work at Ephesus. From there it appears that he journeyed to Macedonia, leaving Timothy behind to carry on the work in Ephesus. Timothy had always been a favourite with St. Paul, but he was still rather young and Paul wrote his first letter to him in an endeavour to see that he did not make any serious mistakes.

I TIMOTHY

Paul first reminds Timothy of the true nature of his task. *i* It is to keep the would-be leaders in Ephesus from teaching novelties. The Law has its good points, but was 8 intended essentially for the lawless. It is not through the 12 Law that salvation comes. Paul himself was saved through faith in Christ and he is thus an example to all sinners. Let Timothy teach on those lines and he will justify the 18 testimonial given him by the prophets when he was ordained.

The following chapters give a series of instructions.

ii   Chapter ii deals with public prayer and says that it should
be offered for all sorts and conditions of men. In such
prayer men should take the lead. Women should be silent
in the services and quiet in their dress and demeanour.

iii   Chapter iii gives instructions on appointments to the
ministry. The qualifications for a Bishop are that he must
have one wife and that he must not be inexperienced in

8   pastoral duties. Deacons should be regarded as on proba-
tion and they should never be ordained unless they are
well spoken of by the people among whom they live. These

14   precautions are necessary because the Church is the pillar
of truth and nothing must be done to undermine its support.

iv   Then comes a warning about the future. The Spirit
has made it known there will be a final apostasy. Teachers
will arise who will go to the length of prohibiting marriage
and insisting on all kinds of taboos. But all food taboos

6   are broken by the grace said at meals. Strict personal
advice is given to Timothy to remember that religion is
a serious job. He must not allow himself to be put upon.
He must remember to stir up the grace that has been given
to him and above all he must stick faithfully to his task.

v   Chapter v tells him how to deal with various classes of
people. He must be respectful to the elderly as to his own
parents, while the younger he can treat as brothers and

3   sisters. Widows should be normally looked after by their
children, but if they are destitute the Church must help
them.

17   Other instructions follow about the Presbyters. Good
work should be rewarded but there must be no favouritism.
For himself he is told to exercise special care and watchful-
ness, but he need not go to the length of being completely

teetotal. He can drink a little wine as an aid to digestion.

Next comes a dissertation on conduct which shows the *vi*
moral code in a much less concise literary form than we
have met before. The opening verses deal with slaves, with 3
scrupulous believers and with people whose only aim is to
get rich quick. Timothy himself is told to fight the good 11
fight, and to fulfil the obligations of his baptism. The rich 17
are told that they must not be haughty but useful, justifying their means by their generosity and aiming at the
acquisition of spiritual wealth. Finally Timothy is told to 20
avoid the temptation to run after esoteric 'wisdom'.

TITUS

On his journey to Macedonia Paul visited Crete. At
his departure from that island he left Titus behind to build
up the Church organization which he himself had only
started. Later, while spending the winter at Nicopolis, his
thoughts evidently dwelt on his friends and the work in
Crete, and he dispatched this letter to give Titus advice
on his pastoral duties.

He begins by affirming that his commission is from God. *i*
This of course would have the effect of strengthening Titus'
belief in his own authority since he in turn had been com-
missioned by St. Paul.

He then starts to speak about matters of organization. 5
He instructs Titus to get on with the work of appointing
Presbyters, and describes the proper qualification for a
Bishop. These instructions are not so clear as we could
have wished. It is not certain whether the terms 'Presbyter'
6

and 'Bishop' refer to the same office or whether the Bishop is the presiding Presbyter.

10   He proceeds to warn Titus against false teachers, who are especially linked with the Judaizers. Their main motive is money. Those who follow them get tied up in all sorts of regulations about ceremonial defilement, when, in point of fact, that has no importance in the moral sphere at all. These people also are always 'against the government', and they must therefore be rebuked with severity.

ii   Chapter ii introduces us to a new version of the moral code. It begins by dealing with the older men and women, asserting that the former must be serious-minded and the latter must be good counsellors of their younger sisters. Youths should aim at self-discipline. Titus himself must be a model of good conduct, serious and not flippant. Slaves must be obedient, loyal and honest. There are no commands for masters or for parents and children, but Titus is instructed to teach that God's grace is given to all alike, and that it should issue in moral goodness on the part of all.

iii   Chapter iii describes the good life. The Christian must be above all co-operative. Nothing will more easily show the contrast between the old life of sinful rebellion and the new life in the Spirit, which Christ's kindness has won for

8   us. We must be forward in good works. What one must really try to avoid is frittering away one's energies in trifling questions. One must give oneself to the big and serious matters. The letter closes with final instructions to Titus to rejoin Paul at Nicopolis as soon as he is relieved of his task in Crete, and to see that the Church defrays the cost of a similar journey on the part of Zenas and Apollos.

2 TIMOTHY

Presently, in 63, or perhaps in 67, Paul finds himself again confined in prison at Rome. His thoughts go out to the young man whom he had left behind in Ephesus, perhaps the closest friend and disciple he has ever had, at any rate the one who drew from him the deepest affection. He writes his second letter to Timothy giving him a few final instructions and urging him to come to Rome as soon as possible.

Paul assures Timothy that he always remembers him in   *i* his prayers, and that he has a special pleasure in recollecting that Timothy represents the third generation of his family to profess the Christian Faith.

He then gives advice on ministerial conduct. Timothy is to stir up the gift of the Spirit that is bestowed upon him, and to show not diffidence but creative energy.

'I,' says St. Paul, 'am in misfortune, but that does not   11 disturb me, because I know that God will keep me to the end. Be careful to guard the tradition that I handed on to you.' The chapter ends with a lament that out of all the Christians who have come from Asia to Rome the only one who does not obviously avoid contact with Paul is Onesiphorus.

He then takes up again the discussion of the ministry,   *ii* showing that it demands real strength of character and that he who follows it must accustom himself to endure hardship of every kind. The best help to this end is to keep   8 in mind the resurrection of Jesus, which was the great evidence of divine power. Even martyrs have found strength to die in this faith. At the same time one should   14

avoid all empty discussion, such as that initiated by people
20 who contend that the general resurrection is already over.
22 Thus we shall find that our lives will have both use and
beauty. Moreover we shall be able to reduce our opponents
to silence by the very mildness of our manners.

iii Chapter iii looks into the future and warns of troubles
ahead. Hard times are coming, therefore avoid all shallow
religion-mongers who have no real depth of faith or sin-
8 cerity of practice. They are like the magicians, Jannes and
Jambres, who set themselves up in opposition to Moses,
10 and whose tricks were easily exposed. We must not repine
if the future does bring persecution, for that after all is
the common lot of Christians. Certainly Paul himself had
had experience of it, as Timothy had seen in the very
beginning of his missionary work. The best way to endure
is to hold fast to the truth one has learned and to remember
the Scriptures in which one has been brought up.

iv Chapter iv provides an exhortation to diligence.
Timothy is to be an insistent preacher of the Word, never
losing an opportunity of adapting his message to the indi-
6 vidual needs of his hearers. Paul's own time is up and he
now awaits the ultimate prize. He has been bitterly
opposed, and is now left without any companion save
Luke alone. Nobody had proved strong enough to stand
by him at his first examination, but still he managed to
proclaim the Gospel even in such circumstances and was
for the time being delivered. Timothy is to make haste
and set out for Rome before the winter stops all travelling.

It will be noticed that these last letters deal with very
different subjects from those which form the theme of the

earlier ones. That is the main reason why many scholars question their Pauline authorship. Nevertheless it may be pointed out that echoes of the old controversies can still be heard in the Pastorals. It may further be remarked that, as the old principles for which St. Paul had fought so hard in his early years became formally established and the work of evangelization gave place to the work of organization, new needs arose in connexion with the steadily growing structure of the Church. It is therefore natural to find a change of subject-matter in these final epistles.

In any case it must be admitted that the correspondence as a whole forms a marvellous introduction to the complete life of the Christian from the first dawning of faith to the last struggle to preserve the purity of its expression in everyday ecclesiastical practice. All is in Christ, in whom is found freedom from slavery, release of creative energy and a guarantee of triumphant immortality.

CHAPTER V

The Teaching of St. Paul

In this final chapter we shall try to give a summary of St. Paul's teaching as he himself delivered it through his letters. It is not implied that this will be an effort to systematize that teaching. As we have already pointed out, St. Paul's letters were occasional. They deal with a precise situation, or are the answer to precise questions specifically posed. Probably the nearest approach that St. Paul made to a systematic exposition of his doctrine is to be found in the Epistle to the Romans, but even that deals with the scheme of salvation under only one, or at most two, aspects, and has little reference to other sides of his teaching.

It is therefore clear that if we wished to derive a system of theology from the Epistles we should have to do what has been done in many expert volumes and take into consideration not only the matters with which St. Paul specifically dealt, but also many *obiter dicta* and casual references as well as many underlying presuppositions that can be found scattered throughout the letters. Instead of that what we propose to do is merely to take the main points with which he has dealt in the order in which they occur, and try to set them in their proper relief. This will probably give a better picture of the writer as well as of his teaching than any elaborate systematization could ever do.

After all, though most thinking men and especially

teachers feel it necessary for their own satisfaction to have in their mind some definite scheme of religion, theology or philosophy, they do not in their public utterances give equal emphasis to every part of it. Possibly there may be sections that they never mention in their lectures or writings. Indeed it is probable that the truths we actually live by, and that seem to us most important, are comparatively few. We like to know how they fit into an ordered whole, but a good deal of that ordered whole we are inclined to neglect. Even the preacher, who, following with faithfulness the varying seasons of the Church's year, is bound to touch on almost every aspect of Christian faith and practice, yet may find himself emphasizing over and over again a few salient points. A famous journalist said that the art of newspaper writing consisted of saying the same thing repeatedly but always in different words, and it is likely that some of the greatest evangelists would give the same advice about preaching.

In any case it is a series of salient points rather than a rounded whole that strikes the reader of St. Paul's letters. This may explain why it is difficult to answer the question whether there is any development in his teaching. Some scholars have answered the question in the affirmative and some in the negative. If by development is meant an actual change of view, the negative is probably the right answer. If, however, by development is meant merely that the subjects that demanded emphasis changed in the course of the ministry, the affirmative would be the correct answer. It is obvious that he does not deal with the same subjects in his last letters which he had dealt with in his first. On the other hand it is not easy to believe that there is any change of opinion between the first and the last letters. It has already been pointed out that, while the main theme of some of the earlier letters (though not the earliest) is the fundamental question of the relation between faith and works, the Pastorals deal almost entirely with questions of Church order. Indeed, as we have seen, this change appears so great that many scholars are unwilling to accept the Pastorals as genuine Pauline Epistles. It can be suggested, however, that the change of subject arises quite naturally out of changed circumstances. In one case St. Paul is dealing with a real difficulty encountered by converts in the transition from Judaism to Christianity, while, in the latter case, he is dealing with newly established churches which need organizing. We may therefore continue to accept both sets of letters as containing genuine Pauline teaching.

Further, the points raised in the earliest letters do not entirely pass out of sight even in the latest. The subject of a final apostasy is important in Thessalonians: it is also mentioned in 2 Timothy iv. Again the general resurrection is a main subject in Thessalonians: it also receives attention in 2 Timothy ii. 8, to say nothing of Corinthians and other intermediate letters. It may also be worth pointing out that the same rhythm occurs in the whole body of the letters as can be found in most of the individual epistles. It is St. Paul's well-known practice to devote the earlier part of a letter to the exposition of some great doctrinal principle and to end the letter with a practical exhortation. That is roughly what occurs in the whole corpus of the letters. We begin in Thessalonians with doctrinal exposition; we end in the Pastorals with moral precepts and practical regulations. This may of course be accidental; but it serves, nevertheless, to bind the body of Pauline literature into a consistent whole, while in no way interfering with the casual emergence of the great themes.

With these considerations in mind we can proceed to enumerate those themes, and to show what were the outstanding articles of Christian faith and practice to which Paul devoted the major part of his attention.

I

The Second Coming: 1 and 2 Thessalonians

The first question that St. Paul was ever called upon to answer in writing was that of the fate of the Christians who died before the second advent of Christ (1 Thess. iv. 13). The answer was that Christ would bring them with Him when He appeared. St. Paul claims that he gives that momentous assurance on the authority of Christ Himself. This may mean that he had received a special revelation on the subject; or he may be referring to some actual saying of Christ, such as is found in Matthew xxiv. 31, 'He shall send forth his angels with a great sound of a trumpet and they shall gather together his elect from the four winds, from one end of Heaven to the other.' In any case Paul asserts that the trumpet will sound, and that at its call the Christian dead will arise. Apparently this means that they will be transferred to the immediate company of Christ who will descend with them from Heaven. The living Christians will then be caught up to meet their fellows descending with Christ through the air, and they will all live together with Him for evermore.

When this will happen no one can say. All that can be asserted is that it will be unexpected and that it is quite inevitable. The practical lesson is that the Christians who are now alive must be prepared; they must be on the watch; and they must be sober, not carried about by undue excitement, but steadily devoted to the task before them.

The subject is treated with greater fullness in 2 Thessalonians. There is a little apocalypse in the first chapter which in characteristic language describes the re-appearance of Christ as taking place in fire. It will be followed by the punishment of all wickedness, while the saints will be lost in wonder at the glory of this final manifestation of divine power. Here St. Paul is at pains to remove a misapprehension. His readers are not to be deceived into thinking that the Second Coming has already occurred. The advent will not take place until there have been certain warning signs. There will be a great apostasy. An antagonist of the Christian faith claiming for himself the prerogative of divinity will be at the head of this apostasy, but a restraining power will prevent the defection from passing all bounds. As we have seen, it is suggested that the antagonist thus described is the half-mad Roman emperor, Caligula, and that the restraining power is his successor, Claudius. Apparently after this temporary check there will be a fresh emergence of lawlessness, but that in turn will be annihilated. Of one thing the readers may be assured, that whatever may be the truth of these special manifestations, the evil is already at work in the world and that Satan, the enemy of mankind, is behind it all. The lesson for Christians is quite simple. They are not to be worried or hysterical. They are not to be so agitated as to leave their present occupations. They must continue to do their work and earn their own living, and so hold themselves quietly in readiness for the end to come in God's own good time.

II

The Essential Gospel: Galatians

Here St. Paul leaves the realm of apocalypse and addresses himself to a fundamental question of religious faith. He is dismayed because his Galatian converts are departing from the simplicity of the Gospel delivered to them by him on his first contact with them. He assures them that that Gospel was not invented by himself, but was given him by a special revelation (i. 12). It had, however, been recognized as legitimate by the principal apostles (ii. 9). It had been delivered by him to the Gentiles and its practical effect had been to make circumcision, as far as they were concerned, quite unnecessary.

The real principle involved was that when they had accepted the Gospel, his converts had become dead to all the obligations of the Law, and had become alive to Christ (ii. 16). Thus the method of their salvation was not to be found in the Law, but in faith. This principle was not new, but it dated back through Christ to Abraham (iii. 7). A definite promise had been made to Abraham that through him and his descendants universal blessing should be bestowed. That blessing was not legally entailed. It could not be conveyed through the Law, which in fact was characterized not by blessing but by cursing, not by gifts but by punishments. Thus the blessing was not confined to the members of a particular race, but was intended to be bestowed on all, of whatever race, who showed their faith by being baptized into Christ. Thus the Law was not in conflict with this series of promise, blessing, and faith. Its purpose was simply to keep sin in check until Christ, who was the proper heir of Abraham, could come (iii. 21).

Those who had shown their faith in Christ and had been united with Him by Baptism had entered into His relation of Sonship to the Father. Such Sonship was in itself evidence that they were relieved from the obligations of the Law. Those who were bound to the Law were slaves, but those who had become sons had passed from slavery to freedom. They must be careful not to return to the former bondage, to those elemental forces of this world under which they had once been bound. The difference between slavery under the Law and freedom under Sonship is supported by the analogy of the contrast between the slave son of Hagar and the free-born son of Sarah (iv. 22).

There is thus, says St. Paul, a clear choice before the Galatians: either they must be circumcised or they must not. If they accept circumcision they must realize that it means putting themselves under obedience to the whole Law (v. 3). They must not, however, suppose that they can acquire righteousness by the Law. That can come only by the inward operation of the Spirit. That is the real meaning of freedom. It does not mean licence to do what you like, but letting the Spirit guide and inspire one's conduct. St. Paul then goes on to contrast the characteristic works of the spirit with the characteristic works of the flesh. He concludes by saying that what is really necessary is a new creation. They must realize that they are made all over again by their association with Christ. In His service they will no doubt acquire scars, but such scars will be far more honourable than the wound made by circumcision (vi. 17).

III

Ecclesiastical Order and Discipline: Corinthians

The Corinthian correspondence starts from the fragment 2 Corinthians vi. 14 to vii. 1, in which Paul lays down the axiom that there can be no compromise between good and evil, and that therefore his readers must not get mixed up with unbelievers and they must cleanse themselves from every taint of moral defilement. Then in 1 Corinthians he attacks the prevalent party spirit and answers certain specific questions.

Partisanship contradicts the very nature of Christianity. True, converts may be baptized by different leaders, but all alike are baptized into the same Christ—and He is not divided. Happily Paul himself had baptized so few of them that he could not be charged with starting a party. He was primarily a preacher, and the very simplicity of his message—the cross of Christ—ought to hold out a possibility of unity for all. It avoided the pedantry both of Jewish religionists and of Greek philosophers. It was not intended for the superior but for the simple in heart. There was nothing of the wisdom or the rhetorical skill of the schools in this preaching. Indeed the so-called experts might look down on it with scorn. It could only appeal to people whose hearts had been already touched.

The Spirit spoke to the spiritually awake (1 Cor. i and ii).

Unfortunately the Corinthians themselves were not yet capable of such discernment, and Paul had had to deal with them as babes in Christ. Their very quarrels were an instance of worldly-mindedness. They must remember that the various sections of Christian converts were all parts of one whole. Their leaders might have different functions but they were all engaged on the same work. One planted and another watered, or one laid a foundattion and another built on it, but they all, Paul included, contributed to one end. In any case they could be sure that the work of each one would be thoroughly tested in the end. So they must not look down on one another or press the claims of their favourite leader. All were one, and Paul's own sufferings for the cause had given him a right to equality with the other leaders. Further he was their original missionary. They must expect him still to exercise authority (1 Cor. iii–iv).

Having thus pointed out the need for unity, Paul goes on to emphasize the necessity for discipline, especially in a case of immorality such as had taken place. They must rid themselves of the evil. They must not even shrink from using the extreme penalty of excommunication. But they must be careful to settle their differences among themselves and not bring them into the secular courts (v–vi. 11). Christian freedom must not be allowed to degenerate into licentiousness. Unlawful sexual union is an insult to Christ. If we are already joined to Him, we dare not join ourselves to a prostitute (vi. 12 ff.).

Marriage, on the other hand, is an honourable estate, and it admits of no divorce. The only exception to this rule is when a Christian is married to an unbeliever who voluntarily dissolves the partnership. The Christian thus set free may in that case marry another Christian. But on the whole it is better not to change your condition. The same rule applies here as in the case of circumcision. Remain as you are (vii).

The same attitude of indifference can be maintained with regard to food that has been used in idol-worship. An idol is nothing at all and it can make no difference to the food. Some, however, scruple to eat such food, and others, if they eat it, may be led into further association with idol worship. Let those then who have no such scruples defer to the tender conscience of the rest. There should be no superiority on the one side nor undue pernicketiness on the other. Let everything be done in mutual forbearance and love (viii, *passim*). Paul concludes this part of his letter with a section on the rights of an apostle, including marriage and maintenance (ix).

The remainder of the Epistle is devoted to matters of deeper doctrinal significance. Chapters x and xi deal with the Sacraments. These had been foreshadowed in the desert wanderings of the Israelites, Baptism being prefigured in the cloud and the Eucharist in the life-giving water from the rock. Christian Sacraments must not be confused with pagan rites, and Christians must stick to their own sacred meal. Each religion has its altar, and Christians must be satisfied with their own (x). As for the Lord's Supper, it is not an ordinary meal or an occasion for jollification. It is a sacred meal and has its own proper form of celebration. That form, which has behind it the Lord's own authority and includes His own words of thanksgiving, Paul had handed on to them and they should not depart from it. By this means they will continue the proclamation of the Lord's death until He comes again. It is therefore most important that they should prepare thoroughly for this sacred rite and that they should not mix it up with their customary full meals (xi. 20).

'One minor point. The question of head-gear in church has been exercising some attention. My ruling is that men should not be covered but women should. That is seemly and in accordance with nature. In any case do not let disagreements grow among you, but be at peace with one another' (xi. 1–19).

The next section of the letter is devoted to the question of spiritual gifts. These are many and differ from each other. The Spirit is manifested in variety. The fact is that the Body of Christ has many limbs, each having a separate gift for the performance of its own specific function. Each is necessary to the others, and all together make up one body. Some of these gifts are singular and spectacular, but there are others of a more fundamental and universal nature which every Christian should possess. Of these latter the chief are faith, hope and love; and of these three the most vital is love. *Agapē* is revealed not merely in specific acts but in a whole attitude of heart and mind. It is in fact the quintessential virtue on which all others depend. The others are partial and temporary. They point towards some future perfection in which they will be swallowed up. But love is a perfect thing in itself and its perfection is eternal. It will remain an abiding reality when faith and hope, and even knowledge and prophecy, have been fulfilled and have ceased to exist under their present forms. But love is still itself even in eternity. Indeed it is the only ultimate reality (xiii).

The showiest of all the gifts is that of glossolaly, ecstasy or speaking with tongues. It was apparently much admired by the Corinthians. Paul himself possesses it in a marked degree, but he does not rate it highly because it is not usually of any service to anybody but the possessor. There are, however, people who have the gift of making ecstatic utterances intelligible to the multitude. Their services should be regularly employed wherever such utterances are given a place in the public services. A further disadvantage of glossolaly is that if more than one person begins to employ it at once there is an immediate end of decency and decorum. Paul insists on the paramount importance of preserving order in the services of the Church. If people are moved to speak with tongues, only one person must do so at a time. And there must always be someone to interpret. A better gift is that of prophecy or preaching. It is much more common but at least everyone can understand it. It is of real service to others: therefore it is to be preferred (xiv).

Chapter xv deals with the Resurrection. It opens with a summary of Paul's gospel: Christ's death for our sins; His burial, and His rising again. Paul provides us with the earliest evidence we have in Christian literature of the resurrection of Jesus, and it is more ample than that which is given in the gospels. Our Resurrection is bound up in that of Christ. As our death follows from sharing in Adam's nature, so our victory over death is a necessary consequence of our unity with Christ. A general Resurrection of all the dead in Christ will precede the end of the world. Then death itself will be destroyed, and God will be all in all. The certainty of such a resurrection is the only justification for the custom of baptizing for the dead.

7

The nature of the Resurrection body will be not material but spiritual, and it will bear the same kind of relation to our present bodies as fruit bears to the seed from which it is grown. The final Kingdom is spiritual and can only contain spiritual bodies. Those who are still alive when the last trumpet sounds will be instantaneously changed from their present material to their new spiritual condition. That makes us realize that the only sting in death comes from our sin and that when sin has been removed immortality has triumphed.

The next section of this correspondence consists of 2 Corinthians x–xiii. In it Paul answers one by one the charges that were being levelled against him in Corinth. Being personal they do not give rise to doctrinal teaching and may therefore be passed over here.

There is, however, in the earlier chapters of 2 Corinthians a vindication of the Christian ministry in general. These chapters represent the final letter of this correspondence. Paul is thrilled by the change of heart in his converts and speaks with enthusiasm of the glory of the Christian ministry. It is greater even than the ministry of the old dispensation. That dealt largely with penalties while the new ministry mediates a gospel of acquittal. Further, the old revelation was partial and veiled, while the new is completely open and characterized by perfect candour (iii). Paul himself has been free from any kind of ambiguity or duplicity in his teaching. He has spoken out of a sense of inner compulsion. He finds that his spiritual energy increases as his physical powers fail (iv). The spiritual must properly succeed to the material, and that process will continue to the end. This explains Paul's enthusiasm. Its source is the knowledge that his ministry reconciles men to God and thus creates them anew (v). His readers must seize their opportunity and be as openhearted with him as he has been with them (vi. 1–13).

Thus while Paul's main theme in this correspondence has been the need for unity, he has given us a good deal of information with regard to a number of other important matters, particularly the sacraments, spiritual gifts, the resurrection and the ministry.

IV

Scheme of Salvation: Romans

In the epistle to the Romans Paul gives us his nearest approach to a systematization of his teaching. He begins by explaining that the Gospel message is of universal application because there is an universal need. All alike are under the judgement of God, for all alike have sinned. This applies both to the Gentiles, who have shown by their gross licentiousness that they have not been true to such revelation as God had given them of Himself (i), and also to the Jews, who have not lived up to the special revelation contained in the Law (ii). The Jews had been designated the instruments of God to hand on His revelation to others, but this did not mean that any special favour would be shown them if they did not appreciate the real significance of the Law or fulfil its moral obligations (iii. 1–20).

Paul, having thus established the universality of sin, goes on to discuss the bearing of this universal challenge first upon the individual and then upon the race. The

7*

first involves a psychological approach, the second a historical.

To the individual Paul says there is only one means of escape from the universal judgement. That is by faith—faith in Jesus Christ. Not through any observance of a law can a man be saved, but only through an identification of himself with Jesus. There is thus no room for boasting, or for any feeling of superiority, on anyone's part (iii. 21 to end). An example of this can be seen in the case of Abraham. He was put right with God by his trust in Him before ever the Law was instituted. It was promised that he should be a blessing to others. All who would receive that blessing can do so on the same terms, not of works undertaken to earn righteousness, but of simple trust. This is what it really means to be a descendant of Abraham: it is to share his faith (iv). To such there comes a splendid confidence because, being identified with Christ, they are assured not only of immediate reconciliation to God through the death of Christ, but also of final salvation through His life.

The same conclusion can be drawn from the fact that Christ is the Second Adam. As our natural union with the first Adam involved the certainty of death; so our union by faith with the Second Adam ensures our present righteousness, and our ultimate salvation (v). Thus in Christ we have passed already from a state of existence which is nothing better than death-in-sin to a new condition which is life-in-holiness. If we have shared His death we shall also share His life. This new life means new freedom and new joy (vi). It also means release from any obligation to the Law. Our bondage to the Law has been dissolved by death just as truly as the marriage bond is dissolved by the death of one of the partners. We are not to suppose from this that the Law was a bad thing. It had a very real part in God's economy, namely to make men realize the heinousness of sin. By attaching penalties to sin it underlined sin's importance. But it had no power to effect the holiness it taught man to desire. It thus made clear the conflict between their weakness and its ideal, and reduced them to a recognition of their utter impotence (vii).

But what a change for those who are in Christ! There is no impotence there, and no condemnation. They are filled with the free-flowing vitality of the Spirit, they live naturally in that land of righteousness which before seemed utterly unattainable. And their ultimate glory, in comparison with which their present troubles pale into insignificance, is completely assured. Thus they live in hope, confident that everything works together for the final good of those who love God, and certain that nothing whatever can separate them from His love (viii).

St. Paul's second main argument is directed towards the racial aspect of his problem. Granted the universal character of sin and judgement, what are the means of escape from both? The argument is inevitably historical and faces squarely the issue between Jew and Gentile. If God's original revelation was given to the Jews, why were they now being ignored? And why was St. Paul himself preaching to the Gentiles?

Paul first lays it down as axiomatic that God will not break His promise. If He seems to have rejected the Jews it is because the Jewish nation is not the real Israel to whom the promises were given. There was a double line of succession, only one side of which, that through

Abraham, Isaac and Jacob, was the recipient of God's supernatural promise. The other side, that which broke away in Esau, was of the earth earthy. It was quite within God's competence to choose one rather than the other. We have no more right to question His action than has the clay to query the rights of the potter. In any case Christians, whether they are by race Jew or Gentile, belong to the true Israel, and are consequently heirs of the promises, if they have faith. The rejected Jews, the Jews according to the flesh, are those who have tried to gain salvation by the 'natural' way of good works and not by the way of faith (ix). They were rejected precisely because they wanted a holiness of their own and refused the Good News when it was proclaimed to them (x). But their rejection is only partial and temporary. There is, as always, a faithful remnant, an element of the New Israel, within the Jewish race and nation. They are part of God's elect who accepted salvation exactly as the Gentiles accept it—as a free gift. They have been the means of proclaiming the gospel to the Gentiles, and in due course their own countrymen will hear them too. Thus there is no room for boasting on the part of the Gentiles (xi). Neither side can feel superior to the other. We are all limbs of the same body, each with its own function to perform. Therefore we must be as helpful as we can to one another (xii).

On this practical note, which is developed through the next three chapters, the epistle ends.

V

The Person of Christ: Colossians

The Epistle to the Colossians is directed against exponents of 'higher thought' who would have blurred the sharp outline of the true gospel by encouraging a cult of angels, circumcision as an aid to perfection, and a hankering after esoteric knowledge. In reply Paul makes three points.

The first is that Christ was the agent in the work of creation, and that therefore even supernatural beings are subject to Him. Similarly, He is head of His body the Church, and is the creator of the new life which animates the whole Christian society. Also He will be the agent of a final restoration of all things. It is Paul's business to explain this mysterious design of God which has been hidden hitherto, but has now been made plain to His Church (i).

Second, it is of paramount importance to avoid all spurious imitations of this doctrine. The Colossians must not be led astray by any pseudo-philosophical theories about demonic beings. Nor must they allow themselves to be brought again under any kind of bondage to the Mosaic Law. Through their unity with Christ they have died to all such pettifogging regulations and vapourings of 'wisdom'. In any case such maunderings have no kind of power to check even the most obvious forms of vice (ii).

Third, they must realize that they already enjoy a new life in Christ. They have not only died, but also risen, with Him. They must be careful to live on the higher level to which they have been raised. Let the flesh and its

vices die, and let the readers show the quality of the new
life in the harmony of their mutual concord (iii). The
epistle ends with a moral code (iii. 18) and some personal
greetings (iv. 7).

VI

God's Secret, the Church: Ephesians

Paul here sets out his view of the plan by which God
has been working out His purpose in history, and of the
part the Church has to play in that scheme. Paul was
dealing with a mixed society of Jews and Gentiles. He
must find some way of justifying their existence in a
common organization. They offered a rather nondescript
appearance to the outsider, and they suffered attacks from
both Jew and Gentile, each of whom could give a clear
and succinct account of his own position. How could St.
Paul vindicate the Church?

The fact is that God has had a particular purpose in
mind from all eternity. In that purpose we have a place.
We were actually pre-selected in Christ before the foundation of the world. We were intended to be adopted into
His family, and it is to us that He has revealed His secret.
'His purpose was to make all history work out towards
one culminating moment, when He could bring every
movement in the whole universe, spiritual as well as
material, to a head in Christ.' In the working out of this
purpose both Jews and Gentiles have a share. About this
we all require fuller knowledge, but we already know
that God has shown His power in saving Christ from the
dead and exalting Him to the throne of the universe.
Christ still functions on earth through His body the

Church, which is an universal means of expression for His universal Personality (i). Neither Jew nor Gentile has any merit in this matter. Both have sinned and become fit objects of the divine wrath. But Jesus has not only offered us the free gift of salvation, He has also broken down the middle wall of partition between Jew and Gentile and made us one family in Himself (ii). Thus is the great purpose revealed.

Of this glorious secret St. Paul proclaims himself the exponent. It had been made known to him by special revelation. The gist of it is that Gentiles have become with the Jews fellow-sharers in the promises given through Christ. This is now being proclaimed by the Church, through whose instrumentality even the supernatural world is gaining fresh insight into the ways of God with men (iii). Within the Church we must show our appreciation of this knowledge by living out the new life with all its virtues, and especially by maintaining spiritual unity. This we are the better able to do because in His ascension Christ gave varied gifts of ministry to the Church, so that all our spiritual needs can be met. In such an environment the individual can grow to full Christian maturity, leaving behind all the old paganism and its perverse views (iv). Further conduct proper to the new life is explained in chapter v leading up to a Moral Code (v. 22–vi. 20).

VII

The Glory of the Gospel : Philippians

After expressing his thanks to the Philippians for all their kindness to him and praying that their love may lead to fuller knowledge and appreciation of all the best things, Paul, who is writing from prison, tells them that his misfortunes have fallen out to the benefit of his evangelistic work. Whatever be his own fate, he is sure that he will be able to assist still further in forwarding the Gospel, and from this he concludes that he will be permitted to visit his beloved readers again. Let them therefore rejoice and show steadfast courage (i).

They must also maintain peace and unity by showing humility towards one another. In so doing they will be following the example of Christ, who did not cling to the glory He shared with God, but laid it aside in order that He might become a slave and die a malefactor's death for the salvation of man. 'As compensation for this humiliation God has ennobled Him and given Him a title above all others.' In response to all that has been thus done for them the Philippians must 'work hard for their own salvation with meticulous reverence' (ii. 1–18).

After referring to the work of Timothy and Epaphroditus Paul adds a long postscript on the people his readers are especially to avoid. These fall into two classes, Judaizers and antinomians. As for the former the ludicrous character of their claim is shown by the case of Paul himself. He had all the advantages the Law could give and was in a better position to claim racial privilege than any of them. Yet he had gladly forfeited every material advantage for the sake of Christ. The only kind of righteousness he now aims at is that which is received as a free gift from Christ. He is quite sure that that will lead him to the prize of Heaven (iii. 1–15).

As for the antinomians, they are really aiming at nothing but the satisfaction of their own immediate selfish desires. The best way of avoiding their traps is to imitate Paul's own style of living. As colonists from Heaven Christians must reproduce here upon this earth the culture of their true home. From there Jesus will one day come and transform our earthly bodies to make them like His own glorified body (iii. 17 to end).

In conclusion the Philippians are told that they must keep up their spirits and let their mind dwell on all the best and noblest thoughts (iv).

VIII

Church Order: the Pastorals

The Pastoral epistles are addressed to two of St. Paul's delegates, to whom he had entrusted the organization of certain churches. They naturally deal with questions of order and do not offer much scope for doctrinal teaching. There are, however, incidental references which make it clear that the writer still has his old controversies in mind. Thus in the first chapter of the earliest of these letters we find Timothy being warned against yielding to any 'novelties' in Christian doctrine. Then, after detailed regulations with regard to worship and a statement of the correct qualifications for the ministry in chapters ii and iii, there comes a warning of an approaching apostasy. This will be instigated by false teachers who will prohibit marriage and certain kinds of food. Such teaching is clearly contrary to true Christian doctrine, which is that everything ordained and created by God is good. Again after regulations about the enrolment of widows and the appointment of presbyters in chapter v, and a moral code in chapter vi, comes a brief final warning against the prevalent type of theosophy. 'Have nothing to do with the meaningless jargon and the nice distinctions of esoteric wisdom.'

Similarly in the Epistle to Titus, between instructions about church officers in chapter i and a moral code in chapter ii there is a short passage on the need to silence the Judaizers. This includes the definite statement that 'to the pure all things are pure'. In other words there is no such thing as ceremonial defilement. Thus at one stroke a great part of the Mosaic Law is swept clean away. This does not mean that the good life is to be without authority or regulations. The basic doctrine, which Titus must teach with full weight, is that Jesus Christ gave Himself on our behalf in order that He might redeem us from all lawlessness, and thus create for Himself a people 'for His own possession, devoted to goodness'. This He does through the new birth of Baptism and the new life of the Holy Spirit. Christians must therefore obey the ruling authorities, keep the regulations, and display the homely virtues in their relations with all kinds of people, avoiding all useless discussions about genealogies of angels and all wordy battles about the Law (ii.–iii.).

In the last of these letters Timothy is reminded that the grace of the ministry is a gift of the Spirit which he must continually 'stir up' in himself. Similarly he must guard the original teaching which was handed to him by St. Paul and is already regarded as traditional (i). He must keep in mind the fact of Jesus's resurrection, with which our own final salvation is indissolubly linked. He too must instruct his people to avoid all useless discussions, and particularly he must combat the teaching that the resurrection is past already. This he must do, not bump-tiously, but commending his doctrine by the gentleness of his manners (ii). The future holds in store many troubles. The Church will suffer much both from false teachers and from actual persecutors. He must hold fast to the truth, and to this end he will be greatly helped by the Scriptures, which will impart the wisdom that assures salvation through trust in Christ Jesus. Let him then be diligent, an insistent preacher, and let him never stop teaching (iii. 1–iv. 8).

Having thus run over the epistles once again we are now in a position to pick out the main topics with which St. Paul dealt, and so arrive at a fair idea of the propor-tion of his teaching.

Thessalonians gave us the two great topics of the Second Coming and the Resurrection. It is surely significant that the earliest writing of St. Paul should thus fix attention on the goal of Christian expectation. It explains why hope is so dominant a feature of the Christian's moral life and character. Existence has a real meaning and purpose.

Galatians gives us the most distinctive element of the whole Pauline teaching, his unique psychological approach to religion. Salvation cannot be earned by meticulous observance of a code or by any amount of good works. It can only be accepted in trust as a free gift offered by God as a result of the self-oblation of Christ. This means of course that the Jewish Law has no binding force for Christians. For them indeed it is no longer relevant.

The Corinthian letters deal with a number of topics. In his choice of them St. Paul was not altogether a free agent. He was to a large extent answering questions that

had been put to him. Nevertheless he would not have
dealt with them if he had not thought them important.
Unity, he says, is a fundamental necessity for the Church.
The rallying point for that unity will be found in the
simple preaching of the cross of Christ. It is to be maintained by the sacraments—Baptism by which we are
united to Christ, and the Lord's Supper which, celebrated
in the traditional manner, links us with the death of
Christ and carries forward our recollection of it till He
comes again, vitalizing us in the meantime as the children
of Israel were once strengthened for their wilderness
journey by living water from the rock. Spiritual gifts,
the chief and most essential of which is love, are meant
not for division but for building up the unity of the Church.
Even in death Christians are not divided, for the resurrection will link together in their spiritual bodies both
those who have died and those who are still alive when
Christ comes again. It is the special glory of the ministry
that it reconciles men to God through Christ and prepares
them for this splendid future.

Romans reiterates on a more sublime level the truths
already enumerated in Galatians. Universal sin demands
universal judgement. The only escape for the individual
lies in faith. Being thus united with Christ he dies with
Him to sin and rises again with Him to a new and glorious
life. That life begins here and now, but will reach its
consummation on the other side of the grave. The believer
has thus escaped condemnation and enjoys a guarantee
of future glory. As he once shared the fate of the first
Adam, so he now shares the glory of the Second. On
the plane of history this same process has been worked out
in successive stages: (1) the original promise made to

Abraham on the ground of his faith, (2) the subsequent training of the Jews through the discipline of the Law, (3) the demonstration of the impossibility of attaining righteousness by that means, (4) the opening of the way to salvation for pagan and Jew alike by the death of Christ, (5) the entry upon this way by all and sundry only on the original ground of faith. Thus are God's promises fulfilled.

The epistle to the Colossians sets the person of Christ in its full cosmic significance. He is not to be confused with any kind of angel. He was God's agent in the creation of the universe, just as He was later the Founder of the Church, and will be ultimately the Author of the restoration of all things in God. United with Him we are freed from the Law and enjoy a new life which expresses itself in an entirely new level of moral conduct.

Ephesians relates this teaching more closely to the Church. The secret of God's ruling of the universe is that He has been training mankind to a recognition of its essential unity. This unity is to be found in one Church for Jew and Gentile alike. Christ has broken down the barrier between them and made them both one, as they are both united with Him and with each other in His body the Church. Of this great secret Paul himself is the exponent, and the work of bringing it to open expression is now carried on by the Church.

Philippians is a rhapsody on the glory of this gospel. Present circumstances may seem to suggest that the fate of Christians is to be browbeaten and persecuted. But the whole teaching of the Incarnation is that the very Son of God emptied Himself of His glory and humiliated Himself in order to save man. For that humiliation He has now been compensated by being exalted to the right hand of God, and in that glory Christians share.

The teaching of the Pastorals is mainly an exhortation to hold fast this doctrine Paul has taught and let it have full weight in actual ministry. There are many false teachers to resist, and there will be even greater apostasy in the future. But Christ's ministers already have His Spirit working in them. Let them hold their people steadfast in the sober conviction of these truths. Then, being lifted above all troubles, they will share the ultimate glory of the Resurrection.

We are now in a position finally to enumerate the main points in Paul's teaching. I suggest that they are six: (i) The goal of history and God's plan for the Universe. (ii) Christ, God's agent in the working out of that plan, who is both a cosmic figure belonging to the eternal sphere and also a historic person living, dying, and rising again. (iii) Faith, the psychological means of salvation, by which the believer acknowledges the claims of Christ and accepts trustingly His free gift of redemption. (iv) The sacraments, by means of which the believer is united to the life of Christ. (v) The Church, at once the Body of Christ —the means of His self-expression—and the society in which believers of every race are joined in unity with Him and with one another. (vi) The whole range of moral conduct, with *agapē* as its ruling motive, which is the proper expression of the life of Christ within the personality of the believer.

Index